BITE
SIZE
ADVICE

Bite Size Advice

A definitive guide to political, economic,
social and technological issues

Paul J. Thomas

GOKO
PUBLISHING

GOKO Management and Publishing
PO Box 7109
McMahons Point 2060
Sydney, Australia
First Edition 2015

Library of Congress Cataloging-in-Publication Data

Thomas, Paul J.
    Bite Size Advice: A definitive guide to political, economic, social and technological issues

    p. cm.
    ISBN: 978-1-61339-811-1
    LCCN: 2015937447
        1. BUSINESS & ECONOMICS/General
        2. BUSINESS & ECONOMICS/Government & Business
        3. BUSINESS & ECONOMICS/Education

Every attempt has been made to trace accurate ownership of copyrighted material in this book. Errors and omissions will be corrected in subsequent editions, provided that notification is sent to the publisher.

The views expressed in this publication are those of the author and not necessarily those of Gateway Credit Union Ltd.

To my wonderful parents, Paul and Dorothy Thomas,
exemplary role models of hard work and principled living.

Acknowledgments

A book is rarely the work of one individual and this book is no exception. Many people helped me on the long journey to get *Bite size advice* published. This book, however, owes particular recognition to four women, without whose support it would not exist.

My biggest debt of gratitude goes to my publisher, Katherine Owen. Turning a blog into a book requires a publisher with an open mind who can think outside the square. I hit the jackpot with Katherine. She is a regular reader of my blog and believed it would appeal to a wider audience.

Special thanks must go to Gateway's Chairman, Catherine Hallinan, who also demonstrated strategic foresight and saw the potential in transforming the repository of blog content into a published book format. She championed my transition from blogger to author and was unwavering in her support.

Not to be forgotten is the assistance of my PA, Marisa Dul, who for the past seven years has proofread each blog post before it has gone live on the Gateway website. She also proofread the manuscript for this book. Marisa is a quiet achiever who effectively manages me as well as my busy diary.

Finally, my deepest appreciation is reserved for my wife, Beverley Thomas. Given the pressures of my working week, I write most blog posts at home on a Saturday afternoon. Beverley has encouraged me to do this even though it takes away from our time together. Her support is invaluable.

This book contains a cross-section of blog posts organised thematically into four chapters. Each chapter contains posts covering a common theme. By arranging the posts into discrete subject areas, the reader is able to find all the content about a specific topic in one chapter, making browsing by interest much easier. Note that the chapters can be read in any order and that each chapter begins with a brief introduction. Please also note that the posts contained in each chapter are not presented in chronological order. Each post ends with a footnote showing the original publishing date to provide a timestamp and historic context.

Contents

You cannot open a book without learning something.

-CONFUCIUS

Foreword

It is estimated that there are over 150 million blogs on the Internet and the number continues to rise. The blogosphere has rapidly become a big and busy world, yet is still relatively new. The first blog was written by a college student in 1994 and a decade later the word blog was declared word of the year by Merriam-Webster.

While there are many blogs, not all are created equal. One which stands out from the crowd is a thought-provoking and eclectic blog written by Paul Thomas. Paul is the Chief Executive Officer of Gateway Credit Union in Sydney. Gateway was a relatively early adopter of blogging and maintains one of Australia's leading business blogs.

Australian companies remain cautious about embracing social media tools like blogs. In contrast, Paul has been putting a human face to Gateway via his CEO Blog since March 2008. Paul is living proof that blogging is no longer the sole realm of geeks and believes that corporations without blogs are faceless entities.

This book is a compelling collection of some of Paul's blog posts – 100 to be exact. His weekly posts are a combination of economic commentary, thought leadership and financial hints. What ties these seemingly disparate categories together is that they are all written through the prism of a banking and financial services lens.

Of course, you can't talk about banking without talking about money since the two are so intertwined. Paul has written about the history of money, the future of money and the creation of money. He has also published posts on money etiquette, money disorders and money management.

Money comes in many forms and Paul has explained the workings of fiat money, credit money and virtual money. He has also outlined how money affects Wall Street and Main Street and how money and debt are two sides of the same coin. He has also described the operation of monetary policy and the use of quantitative easing.

As a business blogger, Paul is not an uncritical apologist for free markets because no economic or political system built by humans is perfect. But as an economic rationalist, Paul is proud to nail his colours to the mast and declare that he remains a proud supporter of open markets – even with their imperfections.

To this end, he has published blogs in defence of globalisation, deficits and bailouts. He has stood up for free enterprise and capitalism while underscoring the need for greater ethics and accountability in banking and highlighting the pitfalls of over-regulation.

Along the way, he has pointed out the dangers of excessive leverage, the importance of savings and the need to educate our children and young adults in money matters. From Islamic banking to fractional reserve banking, Paul educates and informs in an easy-to-understand and entertaining way.

The Global Financial Crisis provided Paul with a rich source of developing and unfolding events to comment upon. He explained both the cause of and response to the crisis. The crisis exposed the greedy and destructive side of human nature at both an institutional and individual level.

Paul has a deep understanding of the human condition and is passionate about people and human behaviour. That passion finds expression in the humanistic narrative thread that weaves seamlessly through his blog. Economics is the study of human behaviour as it applies to money and Paul's musings on money and life have touched a chord with a growing readership.

This book's strength lies in its accessibility. Each blog post is succinct and can therefore be digested quickly and easily. This compendium, then, is perfect for the time-starved reader and for those with short attention spans since all posts are concise yet informative.

By avoiding excessive jargon and clearly explaining key concepts, *Bite size advice* de-mystifies key issues which impact our day-to-day lives. It fills a gap in the literature on contemporary political, economic, social and technological issues in a user-friendly way.

You will discover that Paul is a storyteller who eases readers into complex topics while offering authoritative insights and opinions. I am an avid reader of Gateway's CEO Blog which Paul religiously updates every Monday morning to keep it fresh and relevant.

Under Paul's leadership, Gateway has grown from an institution with little brand recognition to a respected name in the financial services sector. He is passionate about Gateway's *"people helping people"* philosophy and believes that credit unions must constantly change while forever staying the same.

Paul has had a long and successful career in financial services. He is a resourceful and strategic CEO who has forged a reputation as a thought leader. An accomplished public speaker and writer, Paul's credentials include an MBA and a Diploma in Financial Services.

In the pages that follow, you will find an informative collection of Paul's blog posts. Persuasive in argument and wide in sweep, they offer a fascinating window into many of the contemporary political, economic, social and technological issues facing society. I hope that you enjoy reading them as much as I did.

C. M. Hallinan
Chairman
Gateway Credit Union Ltd
Sydney, February 2015

Introduction

Never in my wildest dreams did I think my blog posts would one day be turned into a book. When I took my first uncertain steps as a rookie blogger in March 2008, I thought I would quickly run out of steam. Seven years later, I can safely say that my concern was unfounded.

I took to blogging like a duck to water and have never missed a weekly posting, even though I still lose sleep worrying about the content of next week's blog! I find blogging extremely rewarding since it enables me to show a more human side to banking and finance.

From the outset, I have used my blog to offer what I hope have been enlightening insights into the often misunderstood world of banking and finance. I have tried to shine an instructive light on the inner workings of a sector that touches the daily lives and wallets of billions of people around the world.

Whether it's taking out a mortgage to buy a home, obtaining capital to start a business, transferring money to electronically pay bills, putting savings away to fund one's retirement or insuring your life and personal possessions, the financial services industry plays a key role.

Indeed, the financial services industry is the hub of an economy, facilitating the productive flow of funds between sectors, companies and individuals. The banking industry plays a critical role in fuelling economic growth by providing credit to households, businesses and governments.

Money, of course, is a central component of our lives and influences practically every decision that we make. We need money to pay for our basic needs (food, clothing and shelter) and to finance our non-essential wants (exotic holidays, luxury cars and designer goods).

Some people are defined by money, others see money as merely a means to an end while others still have very little money. This economic inequality has driven me to opine on the extremes of wealth and poverty, highlighting the gap between the richest and poorest in society.

Humans love to debate and argue their point. Some of the high profile debates that I have weighed into include the population debate, the climate debate, the welfare debate and the privatisation debate. On a lighter note, I also debated the merits of maintaining a corporate wardrobe.

Maintaining a corporate blog has clearly enabled me to share my ideas and opinions on a range of political, economic, social and technological topics. What I have learned along the way is that you have to distil a lot of information into a coherent and cohesive argument or summary.

If the truth be known, I was initially a very reluctant blogger and was dragged into blogging by a colleague who argued that it would be good for Gateway and for me. I now find it hard to imagine my professional life without blogging – it's become part and parcel of my working week.

The golden rule of blogging is that you have to be authentic, so my blog is an online extension of my personality. My overarching aim is to be an honest and transparent blogger who tries to inform and debate in an entertaining way.

In March 2013, I celebrated my fifth anniversary as a blogger which caused me to look at the blog with fresh eyes. What struck me is that my blog, unlike most others, did not have a name. Choosing a personal blog title is something I overlooked when my blog was launched.

I was told that the best blog titles are short, compelling and easy to find in search results. So, I chose to name my blog, *Doubting Thomas*. The term Doubting Thomas can be viewed in a negative or positive light depending on whether you are a destructive cynic or a constructive sceptic and I am the latter.

Cynicism is a mind-set of automatic doubt whereas scepticism employs critical thinking to determine validity. The word sceptic is from the Greek word *skeptikos* which means to inquire or find out. It is said that scepticism (factual analysis) is the best way of seeking the truth.

The French mathematician, scientist and philosopher, René Descartes (1596-1650), insisted on thinking for himself rather than simply accepting what he had been taught. He resolved to hold nothing true until he could be absolutely certain of it.

Descartes eventually discovered that the one thing he could never doubt was the fact that he himself existed, since the very act of doubting required a doubter. He expressed this conclusion in the now famous Latin phrase *"Cogito, ergo sum"* – I think, therefore I am. To paraphrase Descartes – I think, therefore I blog.

Finally, please note that each blog post was originally written to be read independently of the rest. Given this fact, some repetition and overlap occurs when stand-alone posts covering the same topic – albeit from different angles – are reproduced together in this one book.

01.
political

Like it or not, you can't escape politics. Every day around the world, governments make decisions that affect our day-to-day lives. Politicians determine how much tax we pay, what laws we obey and how much money the state spends on essential services like roads, education and healthcare. The blog posts in this opening chapter examine public policy in a range of areas including regulation, competition, trade, privatisation and globalisation. There's also a comment on government bureaucracy and the need to eliminate red tape.

In defence of bailouts

At the height of the Global Financial Crisis (GFC) in 2008, the world was on the edge of an economic precipice. Financial markets were in meltdown, global banks were on the cusp of failing and powerful shockwaves were being felt around the world.

Faced with financial Armageddon, governments moved to rescue the troubled banking system. Household names like Citigroup and Bank of America were in a state of peril. Lesser known institutions like Fannie Mae and Freddie Mac were also in distress.

Governments, quite rightly, could not sit idly by and watch their banking systems crash. If banks were allowed to go under, the damage to national economies would have been incalculable. Bailouts were, therefore, used as a circuit breaker to mitigate contagion risk.

The risk of contagion in banking, also called systemic risk, is akin to a chain reaction. Bank failures create a domino effect. Financial difficulties at one bank can quickly spill over to other banks or the financial system as a whole, resulting in a wave of distressed institutions.

The GFC starkly revealed how interconnected the financial world has become. Problems in the US subprime mortgage market spread rapidly to other parts of the market and impacted the stability of institutions everywhere. This ripple effect had the potential to fell both solvent and insolvent banks.

Contagion arises because banks are financially exposed to one another, both through the payments system and through other types of activities such as loans and derivatives. These balance sheet linkages (or interbank liabilities) between financial institutions mean that they are too interconnected to fail.

Banks and other financial institutions play a critical intermediation role in the economy. They act as an intermediary (go between) in moving money between investors and borrowers. Put another way, banks act as a middleman between suppliers of funds and users of funds.

Moreover, banks clear cheques, settle ATM transactions and effect electronic transfers and other payments. No banking activity is as fundamental to society as payments. The list of payment instruments includes debit cards, credit cards, direct debits, direct credits and Internet banking.

Not to be forgotten is the role of banks in credit creation. Banks create money through their lending activities. When a bank makes a loan to a customer and deposits the proceeds into a bank account, new credit money is created.

Money borrowed from a financial institution increases the money supply. A distressed banking system provides reduced credit which results in a lack of money (credit squeeze) for the rest of the economy. Without access to capital, businesses contract and unemployment rises.

Virtually every business and individual in the world has a bank (or credit union!) account. Modern trade and commerce would be almost impossible without the availability of banking services. This is why governments acted in unison to bring stability to the global banking system.

Not every distressed institution received a bailout. Both in Australia and abroad, authorities arranged "shotgun marriages" with stronger institutions taking over ailing competitors at knockdown prices. Examples include JP Morgan's buyout of Bear Stearns and the acquisition of BankWest by the Commonwealth Bank of Australia.

Many people remain angry that taxpayer funds were used to prop-up the banking sector. Citizens around the world are unhappy that they had to pay for the mistakes and oversights made by banks. However, as I outlined above, rescuing troubled institutions was the lesser of two evils.

The public backlash to what many saw as rewarding bad behaviour is understandable. I too feel annoyed. Smaller financial institutions, like credit unions, did nothing to bring about the financial crisis. Yet we now face increased regulation because of the cavalier behaviour of others.

Posting Date: 4 February 2013

In defence of globalisation

The car that I drive was made in Japan. The watch that I wear was made in Switzerland. The suit that I don was made in Malaysia. The iPhone that I use was made in China. Like all Australians, I have access to a wide range of affordable yet quality products. I benefit from the lower price of these items since they are made more cost-effectively overseas.

But what if the government told Australians that they could no longer buy imported goods. I suspect there would be riots in the streets as globalisation impacts our everyday lives. Australians would no longer be able to spray French perfumes, drive German cars, self-assemble Swedish furniture or watch flat-screen televisions from Korea.

The strongest argument for globalisation is that it enables you to profit from specialisation. For example, the Chinese are very good at producing low-cost goods. Economists refer to this as a *comparative advantage*. China's comparative advantage is due to its cheap labour and low production costs.

As a result, China has an edge in making clothes and, Ralph Lauren, the designer of the uniforms for the 2012 US Olympic team, arranged for the uniforms to be manufactured in China. Predictably, some US senators engaged in populist politics and were up in arms that American athletes had to don "Made in China" uniforms.

There was outrage on Capitol Hill with calls to "burn the uniforms" and that it was "embarrassing" for the athletes to wear them. For my money, these comments reflect a lack of understanding of comparative advantage and how trade works. A *Forbes Magazine* contributor put it well in saying that "someone should tell these folks that if you want to have exports, you also have to have imports"!

The reality is that the Made in China uniforms were good for the US economy and for US jobs. In the lead up to the London Olympics, a blogger for *Bloomberg Business* explained it this way:

> Garment manufacturing is a low-cost commodity business. Most of the value in the apparel industry comes from design, technology, sales, marketing and distribution – not manufacturing. The successful players in apparel, such as Ralph Lauren and Nike, figured this out long ago. ...But just because America doesn't manufacture apparel anymore doesn't mean we can't lead the industry.
>
> In fact, the world's largest apparel companies are almost all US-based, including Nike, (and) ... Ralph Lauren, to name a few. ...Nike has created more than 15,000 new jobs in the US (during the past decade), and Ralph Lauren almost 10,000. And unlike the low-paying production jobs next to sewing machines, these are well-paying jobs in marketing, accounting, design, and management.
>
> These companies are winning globally by out-designing, out-innovating, and out-marketing the competition. Nike, for example, is unveiling a new TurboSpeed running suit at the London Olympic Games. ...Nike's gear will be used by teams from many countries, including Russia, China, and of course, the US. What Nike and Ralph Lauren don't do is make their own products, in the US or elsewhere – and this has become their competitive advantage.

It's clear that the Chinese are good at producing low-cost garments. The US, on the other hand, is good at innovation and design, software and medical equipment. Meanwhile, Japan has a highly skilled labour force that uses technologically advanced equipment to produce cars and electrical equipment.

The Italians, of course, are known for their fabrics and fashions. And Australia exports its raw materials to the world. We have an abundance of natural resources that we cannot use and are able to sell the surplus to other countries, giving us a world market of over 7 billion people.

Everyone benefits when countries specialise in the type of production at which they're relatively most efficient. This includes the millions of people in emerging markets who have climbed out of poverty because of the free flow of goods and services across borders.

Regrettably, this fact is often overlooked by the anti-globalisation protest movement. Ironically, these activists are more than happy to use the outputs of globalisation – cheap cars, low-cost electrical items, affordable designer clothing and iPods to name a few.

What the protesters fail to understand is that global free trade promotes economic growth, creates jobs, makes companies more competitive and lowers prices for consumers. Free trade is a global economic engine which is the biggest eliminator of poverty and creator of opportunity that the world has ever seen.

Posting Date: 12 November 2012

Should governments privatise?

Margaret Thatcher started doing it in the late 1970s. Ronald Reagan jumped on the bandwagon in the early 1980s. The Japanese followed suit in the mid-1980s. Now everyone's doing it – privatisation is sweeping the world. Both developed and developing nations are divesting themselves of government owned enterprises including railroads, airlines and telecommunications.

The motivation to privatise is typically driven by a combination of three factors: (a) the desire to raise cash to retire government debt; (b) the need to reduce subsidies to profit-losing state enterprises; and (c) the hope that private investors will bring managerial practices and technology to upgrade utilities.

In the extreme, privatisation results in the transfer of ownership and control of state services and enterprises to private ownership. But more common are public-private partnerships in which the facilities are still owned by the government but managed privately.

Supporters of privatisation claim that governments are bureaucratic, inefficient and incompetent at providing services. Public sector defenders, on the other hand, label the private sector as greedy, unethical and prone to corporate failure. While neither sector has a perfect track record, it's unhelpful to tarnish either with sweeping generalisations.

For my part, I do not see privatisation as inherently good or bad. My contention is that it has to be done right. Privatisation works best when there is vigorous competition among alternative service providers. There also needs to be a clear understanding of which enterprises are best suited for a public-private partnership approach.

Privatisation in Australia started in earnest with the sale of the first tranche of the Commonwealth Bank in 1991. It continued with the privatisation of Qantas airlines (which began in 1992) and has since gained momentum to include the partial sale of Telstra and the sale of Sydney Airport.

Australian governments, both Commonwealth and State, have now privatised a significant portion of the public sector. This includes electricity and gas in Victoria and electricity in South Australia. We've also witnessed the sale of the State Bank of NSW, the State Bank of Victoria, GIO in NSW and SGIO in Western Australia.

Privatisation is not a panacea to public sector woes nor is it a licence to print money for the private sector. While many people worry about the government selling off the family silver, privatisation is an important element of microeconomic reform which is designed to improve market efficiency by limiting government interference in the economy.

Like all public policy debates, the privatisation debate is an emotive battlefield. Politicians, interest groups and the general populace treat privatisation arguments like warfare. Once you pick a side, you're expected to support all of your side's arguments and attack every argument mounted by the enemy side, lest you be accused of being a traitor.

I think we need to be a bit more pragmatic. A case-by-case approach to privatisation is essential – as is an open mind – to the potential social and economic benefits of any asset sale. Transparency is also crucial as taxpayers understandably want to know that asset valuations are realistic and that procedures for calling for bids and evaluating offers are fair.

Posting Date: 14 March 2011

Global banking laws

While on holidays recently, I saw many things which are legal in Europe but illegal under Australian law. In London, I saw crowds of people drinking on footpaths outside pubs. In Dubrovnik, I saw dogs being walked in the lobby of a five-star hotel. In Zurich, I saw scores of cyclists riding on roads without bicycle helmets. And in Frankfurt, I saw smokers light-up in sidewalk bars, cafés and restaurants.

What's right and what's wrong depends on where you are in the world. From how much income tax you pay to which side of the road you drive on, nation-states determine their own sovereign laws. But this is changing. While elected governments still make national laws which are binding ("hard law"), unelected experts are increasingly making non-binding international rules ("soft law") which countries are adopting.

In a globalised world with cross-border trading, the emergence of "soft" international law invariably results from the inadequacy of "hard" national laws. A good example of this is banking regulation. Until the early 1970s, banking regulation was considered the exclusive preserve of national policy makers. However, the collapse of a German bank and a US bank in 1974 showed that financial crises were no longer confined to one country.

It became clear that coordinated international action was needed to prevent shock waves from one nation's problems reverberating worldwide. As a result, the central bank governors from the G10 countries began meeting at the offices of the Bank for International Settlements in Basel, Switzerland. Their aim was to develop uniform international safety standards for banks. The Committee became known as the Basel Committee on Banking Supervision.

The Committee – which has since been expanded – acts as an advisory body and produces Accords (banking regulation recommendations) rather than laws. Even though it has no legislative power, the Committee's members are senior representatives of bank supervisory authorities from around the world and its views hold great sway. The Basel Accords have become the regulatory standards for virtually all nations with international banking activities.

Among other things, the Accords specify the amount of capital that banks and other financial institutions must hold. The original Basel Capital Accord (now called Basel I) was reached in 1988. This had some shortcomings, so a New Capital Accord (Basel II) was released in 2004. Neither Basel I nor Basel II prevented the Global Financial Crisis. Therefore, a third Accord – Basel III – was endorsed by the G20 Leaders in 2010.

Few see the new set of Basel III regulatory requirements, which will be phased in globally from 2013, as a panacea. Notably, Mervyn King, governor of the Bank of England, believes "Basel III on its own will not prevent another crisis" and that the new levels of capital are insufficient to avoid a further disaster. The harsh reality is that no set of rules can ensure the solvency of the banking system or its resilience in a crisis. Like driving a car, banking involves risks which can't be totally eliminated.

Banking regulation will continue to evolve, punctuated by bursts of activity every time that there is a serious crisis to manage. In broad strokes, my contention is that the likelihood of future crises can be reduced through better risk management systems and strengthened governance processes – two things which are continually under the spotlight at Gateway.

I'm conscious that the Basel Accords seem obscure and irrelevant to people outside banking. Yet they are the backbone of the financial system and are designed to protect depositors' and taxpayers' money. In Australia, we are fortunate that our banks, building societies and credit unions are well-managed and well-regulated. Australian depositors have good reason to be confident in their financial institutions.

Posting Date: 12 September 2011

Explaining political leanings

I understand the difference between up and down. I also know the difference between north and south. But when it comes to left and right in a political sense, I'm less clear. What does it really mean to be left-wing? How does this differ from those who lean to the right?

The terms left-wing and right-wing define opposite ends of the political spectrum. Yet, there is no firm consensus about their meaning. Over time, these labels have become blurred. Former British Prime Minister, Tony Blair, once argued that the distinction between the two had melted away into meaninglessness.

The genesis of the terms "left" and "right" date back to eighteenth century France and the French Revolution. Members of the First General Assembly were seated according to their political orientation. Supporters of the king sat to the right of the Assembly president with supporters of the revolution to his left.

In line with this historic division, contemporary left-wingers are said to be anti-royalists who favour interventionist and regulated market economic policies. Right-wingers, on the other hand, are said to be monarchists who favour laissez-faire, free market economic policies.

In Australia, the Labor Party has traditionally been seen as left-wing (socialist) with historic ties to the union movement. The Liberal Party has customarily been considered as right-wing (capitalist) with long-standing ties to the business community. Many see these labels as outdated in describing Australia's modern political landscape.

Take, for example, the issue of Australia becoming a republic. Based on traditional ideology, you would expect this cause to be championed by the "anti-royalist" Labor Party. Yet the push for a republic has been spearheaded by a member of the "monarchist" Liberal Party.

Liberal frontbencher, Malcolm Turnbull, is a Liberal blue-blood. (Note: Left-wing parties are typically associated with red, the colour of revolution, while right-wing parties are often associated with conservative blue.) Turnbull is a millionaire former investment banker who, uncharacteristically for a conservative politician, is also a staunch supporter of the Australian Republican Movement.

In trying to discard the monarchy, Turnbull was seen to take a left-wing stance which caused some right-wing hardliners to label him a turncoat. But he is not the only politician to be off course in a strict ideological sense. Former Labor Treasurer, Paul Keating, lurched to the right economically.

Keating's laudable economic reforms included deregulating the financial system, floating the dollar, reducing import tariffs and introducing compulsory superannuation – things that a Labor Treasurer was not expected to do. It is said tongue-in-cheek that Keating was Australia's best "Liberal" treasurer and the architect of neo-liberalism in Australia.

Many of Keating's reforms were based on the 1981 Campbell Inquiry Report into Australia's financial system. John Howard commissioned the inquiry when he was Liberal Treasurer. But Howard disappointed his traditional supporters – capitalists – by implementing only one of Campbell's 260 recommendations.

Ironically, it was Keating, post-1983, who introduced many of the Campbell recommendations. He implemented a globalisation agenda which made Australia internationally competitive and opened our economy to the rest of the world. Not surprisingly, big business embraced Keating – even though the Labor Party and corporate Australia are supposed to be adversaries.

So, how left-wing was Keating as a left-wing politician? The reality is that he moved the Labor Party to the right of centre. The message is clear: While academics may argue that ideological differences are reflected in the policies of each party, this is not always the case. Voting purely along traditional party lines is now not a guarantee that you will get policies that are classic left or classic right. I believe that we need to shun this binary thinking since it represents an obsolete linear paradigm. Whether you swing left, lean right or aim dead centre, it's incumbent on all of us to keep abreast of the workings of our political system.

Posting Date: 16 September 2013

The media politician

In the lead up to the 1960 US presidential election, John F. Kennedy and Richard Nixon squared off in the first televised presidential debate in American history. The viewing public gleaned little about the policies of each candidate but learned a great deal about their looks and presentation. Kennedy came across as calm and confident while Nixon appeared sickly and sweaty.

As the story goes, those who listened to the debate on the radio thought that Nixon had won while those who watched the debate on TV believed Kennedy came out on top. Nixon's problem was not his debating skills but his staid image compared with the young, charismatic and handsome Kennedy. It is said that Americans were asked to vote "for glamour or ugliness".

The new medium of television caused citizens to focus on image as well as issues which changed the political landscape forever. The movie-star-looking JFK is credited with sparking the political shift from policy to personality. Many believe this shift has gone too far with contemporary politicians seemingly focussed more on likeability than substance.

There's no doubt that modern day politicians need to be media savvy and able to work a crowd. But has the politics of style over substance gone too far? Like many, I believe it has but as I opined in an earlier blog post about political leadership that it's largely our fault since we (as citizens) get the government we deserve.

Many citizens of democracies around the world now vote for the personality more than the policies. I've lost count of how many times I've heard people say they like or dislike a given politician without offering any coherent and rational argument. Political parties have responded by manufacturing images at the expense of providing authentic leadership.

Being a political media darling is one thing but having the ability to truly articulate a clear vision of the future is something quite different. My view is that political leaders can drive change in the face of opposition if they have the courage of their convictions. Regrettably, such bold leadership is increasingly difficult to find in politics.

Politicians have become scared of upsetting the electorate (that's us!) and let opinion polls and minority groups unduly influence policy formulation. This often results in long-term economic credibility being sacrificed for short-term populist reforms. The end outcome is a public which gets policies that are against their own best interests.

An example is our obsession in Australia with national public debt. We have been conditioned to believe that debt is bad and so any political leader who does not pledge to lower our national debt is not worthy of our vote. However, it's a sweeping generalisation to say that debt is inherently bad. Frankly, I would welcome more national debt as long as it is "good debt".

In a previous post, I explained the difference between good debt and bad debt. Public debt which fuels economic growth is good debt. Why then are we as a nation so afraid to borrow to invest in our future? Currently, we need to borrow to build and upgrade essential public infrastructure like roads, airports, sewerage plants, hospitals and schools.

One prominent Australian banker believes, quite rightly, that Australia has a debt problem – we don't have enough to fund desperately needed infrastructure! Nobel Laureate and leading global economist, Joseph Stiglitz, agrees. In an article about Australia's irrational attitude to public debt he wrote:

> Instead of focusing mindlessly on (budget) cuts, Australia should instead seize the oppor- tunity afforded by low global interest rates to make prudent public investments in education,

infrastructure and technology that will deliver a high rate of return, stimulate private investment and allow businesses to flourish.

Most economists agree that the actual amount of national debt is less important than the percentage of debt to GDP. Japan's debt-to-GDP-ratio is 214.3 per cent, the USA's is 73.6 per cent while Australia sits at a low 26.9 per cent. The reality is that we are not heavily indebted, so our politicians should stop whipping up public panic. In Australia, no one needs to be afraid of the Big Bad Debt!

Posting Date: 30 September 2013

Free trade versus protectionism

Long held and deep-seated beliefs are hard to change. Open competition is an example where much of the dialogue is ill-informed. Virtually every economist will tell you that free trade beats protectionism any day. Yet arguments for anti-globalisation (protectionism) continue in political and social discourse.

Over 200 years ago, Adam Smith, the father of modern economics, espoused the benefits of free markets in his magnum opus, *The Wealth of Nations*. Smith argued that it is irrational to produce at home that which can be imported more cheaply. He criticised the idea that protectionist tariffs serve the economic interests of a nation by protecting local industries.

Another legendary economist, David Ricardo, built on the work of Smith and developed the most important concept in international trade – the theory of comparative advantage. According to Ricardo, nations should specialise in making goods they can produce most efficiently (their area/s of comparative advantage) and trade for goods they make less well.

To be clear, free trade is the unrestricted purchase and sale of goods and services between countries without the imposition of constraints such as tariffs, duties and quotas. Protectionism, on the other hand, is the deliberate restriction of international trade by means of government policies designed to shield domestic industries and jobs from foreign competition.

The belief that protectionism can preserve jobs in the long-run is an illusion. The prime example of this is the Australian car industry. Over the past decade, Ford has received an estimated $1.1bn in government subsidies. Notwithstanding this taxpayer funded assistance, Ford is leaving Australian shores in 2016 which will result in the axing of 1200 manufacturing jobs.

Announcing the closure, the head of Ford in Australia said: "Our costs are double that of Europe and nearly four times Ford in

Asia. The business case simply did not stack up, leading us to the conclusion that manufacturing is not viable for Ford in Australia in the long-term". Holden, which has received around $1.8bn in government handouts, is also battling for survival.

It's blindingly clear that Australia does not enjoy a comparative advantage when it comes to car manufacturing. So, at what stage do we embrace this reality and write the car industry's obituary? Throwing good money after bad will not make the car industry self-reliant and sustainable. No amount of protectionism can force consumers to "buy Australian".

Consumers behave as economic models predict in that they acquire what they want, for the best price. Federal Treasurer, Joe Hockey, made this observation last year saying: "People are not buying Australian-made cars because they don't want to buy Australian-made cars, and the cars are not meeting their demands as consumers".

I suspect that there would be riots in the streets if the government told Australians they could no longer buy imported goods. Free trade provides the cheapest goods and services for consumers. (Note: Japanese consumers pay five times the world price for rice because of import restrictions protecting Japanese farmers.)

The harsh reality is that protectionism costs more jobs than it saves. Protectionist laws that reduce consumer spending power actually end up destroying jobs. Free trade, on the other hand, creates more jobs than it eliminates since it allows countries to specialise in the production of goods and services in which they have a comparative advantage.

Over recent decades, Australia has transitioned from a highly protectionist economy to one open to foreign investment and exports from around the world. The creation of this open and competitive economy has led to 22 years of recession-free economic growth. This transition, of course, has not been seamless or uniformly welcomed.

While job losses in one sector are always painful, local production should not be defended from imported competition. Australia operates in the 21st century which is why we can't continue to protect 20th century industries. As the 19th century English philosopher, John Stuart Mill, wisely noted: "Trade barriers are chiefly injurious to the countries imposing them".

Posting Date: 28 October 2013

Who controls the economy?

Politicians do a lot of huffing and puffing about their economic credentials and claim to be able to control the economy. In reality, governments have some influence and, therefore, only some impact on economic activity, but it matters a lot less than people think.

The global economy can be likened to a vast ocean. Each nation-state is free to steer its own ship and set its own course in open waters. But each vessel has to deal with similar headwinds, like the Global Financial Crisis, which cross national borders.

The fate of domestic economies is impacted significantly by what blows in from offshore. No economy is immune from higher oil prices, movements in exchange rates and other seismic changes. Which is why the fate of most economies is largely determined by global conditions, not domestic ones.

In Australia's case, our recent resources sector boom led to a surge in national income from exports. But the government can't take credit for this boom cycle as it was driven by the voracious demand from developing nations in Asia, particularly China, for our raw materials.

Our central bank has more influence over the economy than the government. The Reserve Bank of Australia is independent of the government and has total autonomy over interest rate setting. Monetary policy directly impacts the demand for credit and consumer sentiment.

Interest rates go down when times are tough and go up when things are overheating. It is ironic, therefore, that glory-seeking governments take the credit when interest rates fall (a sign of a weak economy) and nit-picking oppositions are critical when interest rates rise (a sign of a strong economy).

As noted by author, Albert Alla, not only do politicians have no say in the rise and fall of interest rates, they cannot create jobs in the private sector. Moreover, they are unable to force companies to invest in declining industries and can't micro-manage workers in order to increase productivity.

Consumption by consumers, investment by businesses and government spending are the three major parts of an economy. In Australia, personal consumption is the main driver of the Australian economy and represents more than 50 per cent of our nation's GDP.

Personal consumption represents you and me. Collectively, we have more influence on the economy than the government. Ronald Reagan quite rightly noted that "a government can't control the economy without controlling people" and no democratic government seeks to control the populace.

The Australian Government does not interfere in personal economic choices. We are best able to decide our wants and needs. As a result, the government can't stop us living beyond our means. Nor can it force us to spend or compel us to save (except superannuation savings).

We operate an open market economy where people are free, within the bounds of the law, to engage in commerce at their will and their peril. All markets have rules (the term "free market" is an oxymoron) and governments play an important role in setting industry standards.

With regard to economic competition, the Federal Government is the rule-maker, the referee and the umpire – it regulates markets, ensures a fair playing field and enforces the law. Importantly, it also invests in infrastructure.

In short, the government's job is to improve the functioning of the marketplace and not play a direct role in markets. While government interventions to improve market infrastructure such as roads are necessary and welcomed, over-regulation is not and can be counter-productive to the workings of a capitalist society.

It can be seen that our economy is based on the market forces of supply and demand and the economic interactions between millions of people. Our politicians have little control over most things that actually affect the economy. Yet we unfairly hold them responsible for short-run ups and downs.

The way forward is clear: We should stop blaming politicians for our financial woes and our elected leaders should cease grabbing credit for things that are beyond their control. Let's all be honest about the respective roles that we play in the functioning of our economy.

Posting Date: 3 March 2014

Over regulation

Politicians have made an art form of over engineering things. Governments often rush through knee-jerk legislation in response to consumer or media pressure. Yet, sometimes the best response to an event or crisis is to take a collective deep breath and wait until the dust settles instead of making policy on the run.

In the era of the 30 second TV grab, our political leaders are quick to jump on the bandwagon of consumer sentiment and pander to voters and the popular press. However, in their bid to act decisively, governments often behave impulsively and fail to address or solve the underlying issue. The end result is unnecessary regulation on business, the cost of which is invariably passed on to the consumer.

In a recently released report, Deloitte Australia estimates that government regulation costs the Australian economy a staggering $94 billion a year. This red tape, together with private sector rules and regulations, is "...the biggest single drag on our nation's productivity", according to Deloitte. In the report, Deloitte laments the proliferation of new government rules:

> Not even the federal government knows how many rules you are meant to obey. In fact, we don't even know how many government bodies currently have the ability to set rules in the first place, let alone the number of rules those agencies have laid down.

The Report, *Get out of your own way: Unleashing productivity*, also takes aim at business. Deloitte argues that while the private sector needs rules, it has "...overdone it, spawning an entire industry." Australian businesses spend $21 billion per annum on self-imposed rules, which generate a stunning $134 billion a year in compliance costs. "When combined", says Deloitte, "the costs of administering and complying with public and private sector rules equate to a quarter of a trillion dollars a year."

Deloitte notes that a cost saving of just 10 per cent of that total would equal 1.6 per cent of national income. This is an achievable target and one that business and government should set as a goal. However, both the public and private sectors "regulate in haste and repent at leisure, with each additional rule ratcheting up the pressure on our economy".

Alarmingly, Deloitte claims that one in every 11 employed Australians now works in the compliance sector. "As a result there are already more 'compliance workers' across Australia than there are people working in the construction, manufacturing or education sectors", the report states. The rise in new 'compliance workers' is a key reason why Australian productivity growth has been in low gear:

> New technologies are delivering a huge dividend but we're not seeing the gains... 'back-office' workers such as switchboard operators, mail sorters and library assistants have been rapidly shrinking as a share of the workforce, yet those productivity savings have been swallowed up amid the rising cost of Australia's compliance culture.

In any country, the key drivers of economic growth are population size, workplace participation rates and productivity levels. An increase in any one or more of these factors leads to economic growth and improved economic prosperity. Deloitte, quite rightly, notes that one way to improve productivity is to reduce red tape.

Improving productivity is not just important for businesses – it's also linked to higher standards of living for us as citizens. The reality is that if we don't find ways of becoming more productive, our way of life will suffer. Our need to boost productivity by reducing regulation is critical. The time to act is now.

Posting Date: 10 November 2014

Depositor protection dilemma

We all know you can't insure a car for more than it's worth. This is because insurance companies understand something called moral hazard. Moral hazard is a concept saying that people will take risks if they have an incentive to do so. Ergo, if my car is valued at $10,000 but is insured for $20,000, I might be tempted to torch it.

Moral hazard can entice individuals insulated from risk to behave differently than they would if fully exposed to the risk. Examples include tenured professors becoming indifferent lecturers, insured drivers being less vigilant about car theft, protected managers making poor decisions and unemployed workers being less inclined to look for a job while on government benefits.

The subprime crisis is another example of moral hazard. Many US financial institutions recklessly lent money to people with poor credit histories to buy overpriced houses. They deliberately lowered their credit assessment standards knowing that they could package dodgy loans into mortgaged backed securities and pass off the risk of default to unsuspecting investors.

Moral hazard is commonly associated with any type of safety net including deposit insurance. At the height of the Global Financial Crisis (GFC), governments around the world guaranteed the deposits of citizens in banks and other financial institutions. Most commentators believe that this unprecedented intervention was necessary to protect the global financial system from meltdown.

As the crisis passes, the OECD is urging Australia to fulfil its promise to remove its deposit guarantee which, it argues, is a moral hazard. Nevertheless, the OECD acknowledges that both depositors and banks now believe the Federal Government will always come to their rescue in times of trouble.

The belief that a bank is too big to fail represents a classic moral hazard. If the public and the management of a financial institution believe it will receive a financial bailout to keep it going, management – in theory – may take more risks in pursuit of profits. Yet, there's no evidence that the deposit guarantee has actually encouraged Australia's Approved Deposit-taking Institutions (ADI's) – i.e., banks, building societies and credit unions – to behave recklessly.

We have a strong prudential regulatory system governing ADIs in Australia. While there's no doubt that moral hazard in financial services is real, our robust regulation and good practices prove that this risk can be mitigated.

The GFC shows that governments will act to save banks which are too big to fail. This gives our 'Big Four' Australian banks an implicit guarantee and an unfair advantage over smaller credit unions. That's why I believe the current retail deposit guarantee scheme should be maintained after its proposed review date in October 2011.

As someone who is a staunch believer in free markets and survival of the fittest, I can fully understand why the Reserve Bank of Australia opposes the extension of the deposit guarantee. I too accept that governments should not be the first port of call in times of crisis. However, some form of depositor safety net for all ADIs is essential to provide a more level playing field for Australian credit unions and building societies.

The deposit guarantee scheme provides protection for ordinary depositors, fosters competition in banking and doesn't cost the taxpayer a cent. In short, it's a necessary evil if we are serious about the mutual sector being a viable alternative to the Big Four banks.

Posting Date: 6 September 2010

Stop the pandering

Everyone has theories. We all have our own explanation for why things work the way they do. I've had a theory for as long as I can remember and it relates to short-term thinking. Whenever we make decisions based on quick fixes, instant gratification and populism, we suffer long-term consequences. We see this time and time again in politics, business and even our homes.

We all intuitively know that true leadership is not a popularity contest. This is why prime ministers, CEOs and parents must be capable of making unpopular decisions at times. The good news is that most constituents, employees and children will respect you in the end for making the right choice.

To do and say what is right – as distinct from popular – means that you sometimes have to stand alone which takes strength of character. But if you have a clear vision of the future and how it ought to be, then you can drive change in the face of opposition through the courage of your convictions.

Regrettably, such bold leadership is increasingly difficult to find in politics as politicians have become scared of upsetting the electorate. Opinion polls and minority groups now unduly influence policy formulation resulting in long-term economic credibility being sacrificed for short-term populist reforms.

Paradoxically, when political leaders make decisions based on opinion polls they end up being followers, not leaders. They also become reactive rather than proactive. Moreover, inspired leadership gives way to emotive and ill-informed slanging matches.

The end result is the public gets policies that are against their own best interests, particularly those that threaten business. There are many examples of this in Australia. The Australian Retailers Association branded the government's push to ban plastic bags as populist politics.

The Business Council of Australia believes the immigration debate has descended into populist rhetoric, noting that we need continued, sustainable growth to ensure that our children inherit a strong economy. The ANZ Bank boss recently warned that populist policies were spooking foreign investors.

For my money, former Western Australian Premier, Geoff Gallop, got it right in a recent article, *When populism raises its ugly head*, wherein he stated that populism:

> ... prefers nationalism to internationalism, protectionism to free trade and fundamentalism to multiculturalism. Populists want politicians to support "us" as against "them"... They distrust business and support local environmental activism but don't like... the philosophy of economic rationalism.

Okay, here comes the sting in the tail. Brace yourself – it's largely our fault if we end up with poor political leadership. As French political philosopher, Alexis de Tocqueville said: *In democracy, we get the government we deserve.*

We all "have a say" in voting governments in and politicians should be worthy of the people they serve. Equally, we have an obligation to behave responsibly and to avoid short-term community hysteria just because we don't get our way on a particular issue.

For example, when it comes to rising interest rates, I know, politicians know and every first-year economics student knows that they are a sign of economic growth and prosperity. Yet many in the electorate expect the government to say the opposite – and it does – as it knows mortgage rates are a political hot potato. Boy, I'm glad I can speak the truth.

Posting Date: 16 May 2011

Modern day Greek tragedy

Is it a case of life imitating art? We've had the *Big Fat Greek Wedding*, now we've got the Big Fat Greek Debt. Unlike the light-hearted movie, the drama that's unfolding in Greece is a sobering tale of the crippling impact of government largesse and corruption.

This sorry saga – let's call it *The Art of Political Deception* – started long ago. While Greece's economic mismanagement does not date back to the time of her famous sons, Socrates and Plato, it can be traced to the establishment of the modern Greek state in the early nineteenth century.

A welfare state mentality emerged and a marathon of fiscal trouble began that continues to run its course today. The benevolent Greek Government introduced automatic indexed salary increases rather than base annual pay raises on market indicators such as productivity.

The resultant lack of economic growth created few opportunities and caused the large-scale emigration of Greeks to Australia and the US after World War II. With one of the highest rates of emigration in the world, remittances soon became the largest component of Greece's GDP.

Meanwhile back in the homeland, economically incompetent Greek Governments continued to build an oversized and pointless civil service. The average government job now pays almost three times the average private-sector job. Civil servants are also protected by law from being fired and retire with bloated pensions creating the best working conditions in Europe.

The retirement age for Greek jobs classified as "arduous" is as early as 55 for men and 50 for women. According to a *Vanity Fair* article, more than 600 Greek professions have managed to get themselves classified as arduous including hairdressers, radio announcers, waiters and musicians and all receive generous state-funded pensions.

The spendthrift attitude of successive Greek governments is one of the root causes of Greece's current sovereign debt crisis. However, the government is not solely to blame. The Greek people themselves must also accept some responsibility for the country's economic mess since tax evasion is rampant.

Greece's deep rooted culture of tax evasion costs the country about 30 billion Euros annually in lost revenue. Tax dodgers can be found everywhere. Plumbers, electricians and taxi drivers are notorious for not giving receipts. Doctors grossly understate their income while wealthy home owners deliberately lie about owning a pool to avoid paying a luxury tax.

And so ends Act I of our human tragedy. With a short interlude to reflect on the fact that Greece – at both a sovereign and personal level – has been living beyond its means for decades – we move to Part II and meet the third "villain" (metaphorically speaking) in our plot – the Euro currency.

The Greek crisis became a European crisis due to the common use of the Euro. A single currency is only as strong as its weakest link, as the 16 other Euro nations have discovered. Tiny Greece has been dominating the headlines with speculation it could bring down the Euro if it defaults on its debts.

If Greece still had its own currency, it could employ the standard policy of devaluing its drachma to become more competitive and restart growth. Devaluation makes a country's exports less expensive for foreigners and makes foreign products more expensive for domestic consumers. This helps increase exports and decrease imports, thereby reducing the current account deficit.

However, Greece's monetary union with the Eurozone means it cannot follow the devaluation path. So just over a year ago the

European Union put together a €110 billion bailout package for Greece that briefly calmed markets. The IMF recently warned that a second bailout package is necessary to prevent the world's second global financial meltdown in three years.

The crumbling ruins of the Parthenon are testament to the fact that the Greeks have failed once before. This latest tragedy could again leave the country in ruins. How this tragedy ends is still to play out but the cradle of Western civilisation and birthplace of democracy is fighting for economic survival.

Posting Date: 4 July 2011

Government concessions for many

When it comes to decision making, politicians are pulled in multiple directions. The judgments that politicians make can affect thousands or millions of lives. An endless stream of business associations, community organisations and pressure groups lobby governments to influence outcomes.

These special interest groups play a legitimate role in all democratic systems of government. They are an important mechanism through which citizens can make their ideas and views known to elected officials. The ultimate aim of this advocacy is to shape public opinion or affect public policy.

An individual acting alone has little political clout but, as part of a special interest group, can assert considerable sway. Interest groups come in all shapes and sizes, can be transient or permanent and cover a multitude of issues e.g., anti-abortion, environmental protection or workers' rights.

A well-known interest group in America is the National Rifle Association (NRA). This gun lobby is considered by many congressional staffers and lawmakers to be America's most influential lobby group. The NRA has vigorously opposed many legislative proposals for the control of firearms.

In Australia, the mining sector flexed its considerable muscle in 2010 and unleashed the most ferocious lobbying campaign ever seen in this country. Mining powerhouses Rio Tinto, BHP Billiton and Xstrata joined forces to stop Prime Minister, Kevin Rudd's proposed Resource Super Profits Tax from becoming law.

The lobbying campaign cost $22m, brought down a Prime Minister and led to accusations of "rent-seeking" by the mining industry. Rent-seeking is an economic term used to describe attempts to lobby a government for loan subsidies, funding grants, beneficial regulations or monopoly privileges.

Some believe these economic concessions fail to create benefits for the overall society since they merely redistribute resources from taxpayers to special interest groups. With regard to the changes to the originally proposed resource tax, the public coffers missed out on $60 billion in forecast revenue.

One way for governments to create "rent" is by limiting competition. For example, restricting the number of taxi cabs prevents new entrants and protects the profits of incumbents. This rent-seeking enables taxi owners to obtain a greater rent (return) than would be possible in an open market.

Rent-seeking takes many forms. Historically, farmers obtained government help through tariff protection. Similarly, local manufacturers engaged in rent-seeking by securing restrictions on imports via quotas. Brick and mortar retailers now want protection from foreign, online competitors.

A high-profile Australian retail stalwart spearheaded a campaign to have the government impose the goods and services tax (GST) on Internet retail purchases under $1,000 arguing that overseas retailers had an unfair advantage. The campaign infuriated consumers with local retailers labelled as "rent-seeking whingers".

Bailing out banks is another example of rent-seeking as rescuing banks does not create value. Rent-seeking means "obtaining an economic gain at the expense of others without reciprocal benefit". This definition covers any economic activity that expands one's share of existing value rather than creating value.

As profit-seekers (wealth creators), many financial institutions recklessly expanded their lending activities. They lent money to people who they ought to have known could not pay them back. Mortgage securitizers compounded the problem and destroyed value.

This behaviour ultimately resulted in a number of institutions becoming rent-seekers as governments around the world were forced to prop-up banks with taxpayer funds as a result of the Global Financial Crisis. The auto industry in Australia and in the US also received government financial assistance.

Many saw the bailouts as taxpayer welfare for business with citizens angry that rent-seeking corporations were given fistfuls of cash. The US Government was also forced to pick winners and losers. Lehman Brothers was allowed to fail but insurance giant, AIG, was given a bailout.

In the aftermath of the financial crisis, many questions remain. Key among these is whether taxpayer dollars should have been used to bail out banks and other private companies or should they have been left to their own devices and allowed to sink or swim? I'll answer that question next week.

Posting Date: 28 January 2013

Democracy in danger

In a recent post I expressed concern that politics is degenerating into a farce, with short-term popular sentiment increasingly impacting long-term policy formulation. Hopefully, I left readers with a clear sense of the dangers of the don't-offend-anyone politics which now characterises Australian political life.

What I did not focus on was the role of the media in whipping up emotive opposition to sensible social and economic reform. The media, according to Lindsay Tanner, a former minister for finance in the Labor Government, is turning political reporting into a "carnival sideshow" driven by entertainment imperatives.

In his recently released book, *Sideshow: dumbing down democracy*, Tanner tracks the relentless decline of political reporting in Australia and abroad. He describes in great detail how the media manipulates the discussion of substantive issues in ways that entertain rather than inform. "Policy initiatives are measured by their media impact, not by their effect", laments Tanner.

Tanner, quite rightly, asserts that "genuine democracy requires an informed electorate" but bemoans the fact that the media controls access to the electorate. "The media publishes what people want to read or watch and the public demand for serious news is in decline". Consequently, politicians have been pushed into a self-defeating game of feeding the news cycle with stunts.

Tanner notes that as political coverage gets sillier, politicians are forced to get sillier to get coverage. "As politicians need to be interesting to compete in a world governed by the rules of entertainment, they happily collaborate". Yet he believes that Australians deserve much better than the carefully scripted play-acting that now dominates our nation's politics.

Journalists are always looking for quirky and amusing items that divert or titillate the audience. Tanner cites the 2008 presidential primaries where Hillary Clinton attracted saturation coverage for allegedly revealing some cleavage on the campaign trail. "The amount of flesh on display would have barely troubled a middle-class maiden aunt in Victorian England. Yet it was enough for the media to make it the lead news story across the country", writes Tanner.

Tanner contends that the hyperbole which characterises media reporting is blatantly designed to manipulate the public's emotions. He cites a number of examples where the media created unnecessary panic including the Global Financial Crisis, the Year 2K computer bug and the swine flu epidemic. The media reporting of these events produced a public response out of proportion to the threat.

A popular tool used by the media to distort impressions of politics and current events is "selective coverage" says Tanner. "When petrol prices spike, the media go into overdrive. When they fall, coverage is much more low-key." Equally, every time interest rates rise, we see stories featuring struggling families. Yet when rates fall, little is said about the plight of self-funded retirees.

I think that *Sideshow: dumbing down democracy* should be compulsory reading for all journalists and reporters. Some reviewers have rated Tanner's book as "refreshingly frank". Others have labelled it a "scathing critique" of contemporary political journalism. Personally, I'd go one step further and categorise Tanner's description of the media as "alarmingly true".

Finally, and in fairness, I must acknowledge the media's claim that they simply produce what consumers want. As a society, we would rather read about the sordid private lives of celebrities than have a serious debate about the long-term benefits of public policy. Just as we get the politicians we deserve, we also get the media that we deserve. As citizens, we are complicit with falling standards.

Posting Date: 20 June 2011

What fuels petrol prices?

Some things in life are a mystery. Petrol prices fall into that category. Many find it difficult to explain why the price we pay at the bowser fluctuates daily. While most motorists know there is a price cycle, many question why petrol prices shoot-up just before long weekends and holidays.

To understand how the local pump price for petrol is calculated, we first need to look at global forces. Three international factors drive the wholesale price of petrol in Australia – the world price of crude oil, the petrol price in Singapore and the value of the Australian dollar. Let me explain each in turn.

The single greatest factor influencing Australia's petroleum prices is the cost of crude oil which is measured in barrels. The international price of crude oil accounts for around 50 per cent of the domestic price we pay per litre at the service station. Since the cost of a barrel of crude oil has risen dramatically over recent years, so have retail prices.

But crude oil is not the product you buy at the pump – it's simply an ingredient in the petrol production process. Just as a paper mill turns timber into paper, a refinery takes crude oil and earns a "refiner margin" for turning it into petrol. Ninety-eight per cent of Australia's total fuel requirements are controlled by four refiners – Shell, Mobil, Caltex and BP.

The petrol they refine is an internationally traded commodity whose price is largely determined by movements in global markets. Petrol prices in most countries are established with reference to the relevant refined petrol benchmark price. Australian retail petrol prices closely follow the Singapore Mogas 95 Unleaded benchmark, which is the price of refined petrol in Singapore.

The international benchmark prices of crude oil and refined petroleum are typically traded in US dollars. Thus, the value of the exchange rate between the USD and the local currency influences the retail petrol price. The recent strength of the Australian dollar has protected consumers from the effects of higher international petrol prices.

The next factor to be added to our wholesale fuel price breakdown is government taxes. There are two components to petrol taxes – a fuel excise and GST. All petroleum fuels in Australia have an excise tax of 38.143 cents per litre which represents the second-largest component (25-30 per cent) of the price of petrol in Australia. GST is also applied to the total price, at 10 per cent.

When all of the above components are added together, the price is referred to as the *Terminal Gate Price* (TGP). The TGP is the wholesale price for petrol in each Australian capital city but does not include distribution costs and retail margins.

With regard to distribution, once fuel leaves capital city ports it is sent to rural and metropolitan areas. A large part of the increase between retail and wholesale prices is the transport cost of getting the fuel to the bowser which is why fuel prices are generally higher in rural and remote areas.

Finally, competition also accounts for variances in retail prices and this is what drives the daily fluctuations that you see at the bowser. Petrol retailers discount prices to gain additional sales volume. Competitors respond and prices spiral down until they reach unprofitable levels. The market then corrects itself by ceasing or reducing the discounts.

This "normal pricing" holds only for a short while until someone starts the discount price cycle again. The big retailers, Coles and Woolworths, are key players in these price wars. It is claimed that they are killing independent service stations. With 90 per cent of Australian households keeping at least one registered vehicle in their garage or dwelling, petrol prices directly impact most Australians.

Posting Date: 13 February 2012

Regulation gone mad

Is Australia becoming a police state? Do we have too many rules and laws? Has common sense been replaced with legislation? Is the level of regulation unnecessarily burdening business? In answering these questions, let me begin with three examples.

First, my parents have lived in the same house for 52 years and there has NEVER been a car accident outside their home. But that did not stop their local council from erecting a "No Standing" sign in front of their home a few years ago. When my father and his neighbours complained, they were told the bend in the road where they live had been classified as a dangerous blind spot.

Second, at lunch times I swim in a private pool in the city. Last year, following a periodic routine health and safety inspection of the pool by the city council, the gym manager was forced to erect a "No Diving" sign. The new inspector decided that the pool was too shallow for diving, even though there has NEVER been an injury at the pool in its entire 29 year history caused by someone diving into the pool.

Third, earlier this year, the Gateway Credit Union team celebrated the end of the financial year with a night out at Sydney's Luna Park. We had a great time and, for me, it brought back happy childhood memories. But the unsupervised fun I used to have as a youngster was replaced by safety inspectors on every ride. Even the more sedate rides in Coney Island now attract a watchful eye from the ride attendants.

So, let's recap. I can't park outside my parents' home, I can't practise my dive starts at the pool and I can't be too adventurous at amusement parks. Frankly, I'm staggered that I've managed to live as long as I have given my "reckless" childhood. I slept in a cot adorned with lead paint, rode a bike without a helmet and travelled in a car without seatbelts.

Risk is inherent in everything we do but it should not paralyse us from doing things. I compete in ocean swims even though I could get eaten by a shark, stung by a blue bottle, dumped by a wave or caught in a rip current. Please don't tell the authorities or ocean swims might also become heavily regulated – or banned completely!

The serious point I am trying to make here is that it's impossible to go through life or run a business without taking risks. Indeed, it's unhealthy to even try as you'll risk stagnation. Companies which can see beyond risks to the opportunities they present are much more likely to prosper. But what is an acceptable level of risk appetite for a business?

Well, if you are in the business of financial services you cannot adopt a cavalier attitude to risk. In fact, the business of banking is all about managing risk. One of the lessons of the Global Financial Crisis (GFC) is that it's not enough to manage risk *within* individual banks. Risk needs to be examined on a system-wide basis.

Around the world regulators and governments agreed to restructure the approach to risk in the financial sector. The cornerstone of this global initiative to contain risk is an international accord – Basel III – which contains sweeping new regulatory standards for banks on capital adequacy and liquidity.

Basel III was primarily intended for internationally active and systemically important banks. But the same regulatory standards are being applied to smaller institutions in a one-size-fits-all approach, putting smaller players with fewer resources at a competitive disadvantage. The new requirements will drive the cost of regulatory compliance to potentially unaffordable levels for credit unions and building societies (mutuals). This represents a risk to competition.

The efforts by regulators to bolster financial system stability and to avoid a repeat of the GFC turmoil are laudable. Few would challenge the goal of a more resilient banking sector. But care must be taken not to punish those, like mutuals, which did not engage in the reckless behaviour that contributed to the GFC.

At the end of the day, most regulation is a reaction to the last big disaster and, as I noted in an earlier post, *Global banking laws*, no set of rules can ensure the solvency of the banking system or its resilience in a crisis. Like driving a car, banking involves risks which can't be totally eliminated. Let's not unnecessarily burden mutuals with legislation that will diminish competition.

_____

Posting Date: 19 November 2012

A fairer tax system

Albert Einstein once said that the hardest thing in the world to understand is income tax. There's no doubt that our tax system is baffling, which is why more than 75 per cent of Australians use a tax agent. Tax reform in Australia is long overdue – the system needs to be made easier and fairer.

I suspect that most Australians would readily agree to tax reform if it resulted in a smaller tax bill for them personally. Of course, that's utopian and therein lies the problem. We all want governments to raise sufficient revenue to provide common infrastructure but we don't want to individually pay any more tax.

But with a growing and ageing population, taxes need to rise to cover increased public spending. We need more schools, more hospitals, more roads and the list goes on. Without an increase in government receipts, we are setting ourselves up for permanent structural deficits.

The bottom line is that our current tax structure is fiscally unsustainable and we (i.e., you and I) will be asked to pay more – it's just a matter of time. Over the longer term, governments cannot continue to boost spending without addressing the revenue side of the equation.

The low-hanging fruit in putting more funds in government coffers is the goods and services tax (GST). Shortly after the recent federal election, Treasurer Joe Hockey said there would be "no change to the GST, full-stop, end of story". My suspicion is that it will be a second term agenda item.

While no politician wants to talk about tax increases during an election campaign, the government knows that it has a problem. The GST as it stands is no longer a growth tax – household consumption (spending patterns) has softened resulting in GST revenue not growing as fast as it once did.

As a result, like it or not, the GST has to climb above its current flat rate of 10 per cent. As well as increasing the GST rate, I suspect that we will also see changes to the GST tax base. This will likely be broadened to cover "products" which are currently GST exempt including health, education and fresh food.

Being a consumption tax, the GST is classified as an indirect tax and the prevailing rate is low in comparison to most other nations. Conversely, our direct (income) tax rates are high in a comparative sense. I believe we need a shift from direct to indirect taxation to favour the taxing of spending over the taxing of income.

Indirect tax is where a proportion of the money spent on goods is taken, whereas a direct tax is levied as a proportion of a person's income. Taxation schemes can be classified as *progressive* (the more one earns, the higher the tax rate) or *regressive* (those with lower incomes pay a higher percentage of tax).

There are classic arguments for and against progressive and regressive taxes. It's said that progressive income taxes penalise hard work and ambition since the more someone earns the more they pay to the government. The standard counter-argument is that the "rich" should pay more.

Conversely, it is argued that regressive taxes hurt the poor more as they take a larger percentage from low-income earners than from high-income earners. The rebuttal here is that all consumers should pay the same dollar amount (flat tax) regardless of income level.

Putting aside individual beliefs and biases, I repeat my assertion that we are well overdue for a serious debate in Australia about tax reform. We owe it to ourselves and our grandchildren to develop a more efficient and stable form of revenue generation for the continuing prosperity of our nation.

Posting Date: 18 November 2013

Corporate welfare

In 1974, corporate Australia witnessed one of the costliest new product failures in its history. A year earlier, the vehicle manufacturer, Leyland Australia, launched a large family car called the P76. The car was plagued with quality problems from poor assembly practices and was quickly labelled a lemon.

Aside from the quality problems, Australians did not want a petrol guzzling car at a time when the world was in the midst of an oil crisis. Australian car buyers felt the P76 was too big and too thirsty – not to mention its ugly wedge shape – and opted to stick with their Holdens and Fords.

Fast forward forty years and it is now Holden and Ford that are producing cars Australians don't want. Due to changing consumer preferences, we have lost our appetite for home grown cars. Fewer than half of Australia's 15.6 million drivers prefer to buy an Australian made car.

Australia's car market is now primarily composed of cars imported from Asia and Europe. Our local auto sector cannot compete with cars made better and cheaper overseas. Sales of locally made cars are at record lows with Australian manufacturers propped up by government subsidies.

Just like Leyland, Holden and Ford misjudged the market, yet they – along with Toyota – have been enjoying a $5.4 billion aid package to the industry. According to the Productivity Commission, subsidies to the industry have averaged about $550 million a year for the past six years.

The Commission recently recommended that Federal Government assistance to the embattled local car industry should stop. It said that the justification for subsiding car makers is weak and that "ongoing industry-specific assistance to the automotive manufacturing industry is not warranted".

Workers in the auto sector are paid allowances which are more generous than in most other areas of manufacturing. The perks include Sunday pay of 2.5 times the normal rate, 'wash up time' after shifts, paid time to donate blood, cash bonuses and forced plant shutdowns over Christmas.

These uncompetitive work practices contributed to the decisions made over recent months by all three car manufacturers – Ford, Holden and Toyota – to close down their Australian car manufacturing operations. The harsh lesson is that government spending alone cannot sustain an uncompetitive industry.

This also applies to the agricultural sector and the recent decision by the Federal Government to reject a request for $25m in financial assistance to fruit canner, SPC Ardmona. Our national carrier, Qantas, also made a request for government support.

The Federal Government recently signalled that multi-billion-dollar corporate rescue packages will become a thing of the past. "The age of entitlement is over, the age of personal responsibility has begun," warned Treasurer, Joe Hockey.

As I opined in my post, *Free trade versus protectionism*, it's in Australia's best interests to specialise in those things in which it has a comparative advantage. It's clear that protectionism cannot preserve jobs in the long-run and taxpayers should not be subsidising underperforming industries.

Only profitable industries create jobs and while job losses in one sector are always painful, local production should not be defended from imported competition. As a general rule, I believe that markets should be allowed to operate free from government interference.

To be sure, I don't believe in unrestrained competition where one wins at any cost. Governments have a role to play in defining the rules of competition so that it's not survival of the most ruthless or the most deceptive. Beyond that, it's up to each market participant to avoid extinction.

At the end of the day, it's consumers and not governments who really determine business survival. As in the natural world, Darwinian selection should determine the winners and losers in the corporate world. In this jungle, the brutal reality is that some companies will thrive while others will perish.

Posting Date: 24 February 2014

02.

economic

Economics is a social science. It is the study of human nature as it applies to money. Economists analyse the behaviour of individual people and firms within an economy (microeconomics) and examine the economic activity of an entire country (macroeconomics). When it comes to money we do not always make rational choices and, as explained in a number of the blog posts in this chapter, this contributed to the Global Financial Crisis. Other topics covered include household debt, personal savings, interest rates, property prices, money management, GDP measurement and money supply.

Financial crisis defies logic

The academic world of economics may fit neatly into mathematical equations, but does it describe the real world? I think we humans are far too emotive for rational economic models to accurately predict our behaviour. The Global Financial Crisis is proof positive of that.

The dislocation in financial markets was caused by irrational lending practices – saddling borrowers with dodgy (subprime) loans they could not afford. As the loans went sour, markets overreacted and then fear and panic set in. Investor confidence plummeted and everyone rushed to the (stock market) exit door.

The human species was convinced it faced financial Armageddon and this supposedly intelligent herd animal behaved like one of Pavlov's dogs – the market rings the bell and hysteria starts. The great panic was fuelled by apocalyptic reporting from the media which whipped us into a frenzy.

The white knuckle ride has been made even more exciting by market rumours. Nothing like wagging tongues to propel gloom and doom! But if we had acted more rationally, could we have avoided or mitigated the financial system death spiral?

Conditions in financial and equity markets remain jittery. When the dust eventually settles on this damaging saga, teachers of media and political studies will try to make sense of what happened. Hopefully, economists will learn that markets are not populated by rational decision makers.

They might also learn that the really big events in world history, as outlined in the bestselling book, *The Black Swan: The Impact of the Highly Improbable,* are rare and unpredictable. The author argues that economists live in a fantasy world where they believe the future can be controlled by sophisticated mathematical models.

Posting Date: 29 September 2008

Who caused the GFC?

When something goes wrong, humans need a scapegoat. I know that it is perverse, but we feel better when we blame someone else for our woes. Finger pointing takes the focus off our own behaviour and turns the heat on the "real" culprits. Plus, it feels good to play the innocent victim and exclaim: 'It's not my fault!'

The good news is there's plenty of blame to go around when it comes to the credit crisis. The responsibility for the mounting contagion does not reside with any particular group. No one can claim a monopoly on greed and stupidity. Therefore, many in the populace and media are demonizing everyone and anyone.

Chief among the villains are the fat cat CEOs who pocketed huge pay packets while presiding over lax lending. Others blame US regulators for turning a blind eye to an unsustainable mortgage market. Not to be forgotten are the financial whiz-kids who invented the newfangled securities that turned toxic.

But what about us? Do we need to temper our righteous indignation in the knowledge that, as a society, we have become credit junkies? In a recent blog post, I argued that we are living beyond our means. For many, unsustainable expenditure has become the drug of choice.

I think as a society we need to take a long hard look at ourselves. Collectively, we need to take some ownership for the prevailing economic climate. We need to understand that debt is not risk free. We need to save more and encourage habits of thrift among our children.

But most of all we need to stay calm. Markets are driven by sentiment. The most important virtue right now is not to panic. Let's all work together to rebuild trust and confidence and prove that we are not morally bankrupt.

Posting Date: 3 November 2008

Don't amputate the invisible hand

Just as the Chernobyl meltdown did not put an end to nuclear reactors, the Wall Street meltdown is not the death knell of free markets. Financial markets are going through a life changing experience and, like the nuclear industry following the Chernobyl disaster, the financial services sector needs to learn from its mistakes. But capitalism and its alter ego, the invisible hand, will survive the current market dislocation.

The metaphor, invisible hand, was coined by the father of modern economics, Adam Smith. Smith asserted that economic behaviour is driven by self-interest and that purely selfish individuals are guided by an invisible hand to produce the greatest good for all. The credit crisis, however, painfully shows that the pursuit of self-interest does not always lead to outcomes that benefit society overall.

Many consumers understandably feel they have been slapped by the invisible hand and that it, in turn, should be clobbered by the visible fist of government. But it would be a mistake to substitute the invisible hand of capitalism for the dead hand of socialism. Right now, the invisible hand needs a helping hand in the form of government assistance. This is why taxpayers around the world have become bankers. However, this is not a sustainable or desirable position in the long term.

When the dust settles on this saga, governments must revert to being market spectators and not players. The private sector will undoubtedly be subjected to closer scrutiny from the public sector. All markets have rules (the term "free market" is an oxymoron) and governments play an important role in setting industry standards. Care must be taken, however, not to over regulate.

Finally, to lay the blame for the credit crisis exclusively at the feet of the free market is too simplistic. Governments must also shoulder some responsibility.

Posting Date: 9 February 2009

Back to the future in lending

Remember the days when you had to save up for a deposit before obtaining a home loan? A quaint practice, I know, but it was one of the foundation stones of something from the dim, dark past called "prudent lending".

There was no such thing as easy credit when I started my banking career over 30 years ago. As a young credit assessor I had the three C's of credit – capacity, character and collateral – drilled into me. A responsible lender did not deviate from these tried and tested standards.

Fast forward to today and we are reaping the rewards of what we have sown over the past decade. Dubious and risky lending practices have created a Devil's kitchen where institutions have gorged on a diet of toxic loans. The global financial system is still trying to digest a poisonous broth of subprime mortgages and is now starting to swallow a rising number of personal bankruptcies caused by credit card debt. No wonder the system is choking!

For many years I watched with dismay as personal "wealth" was increasingly born of leverage. It seemed as if virtually everyone wanted to "super-size" their debt. That's why I have repeatedly said that borrowers are not blameless spectators to this financial crisis. Many consumers who binged on debt are now suffering a self-inflicted hangover.

I know that it's easy to be wise in hindsight, but greater risk assessment should have been undertaken before subprime loans, 100 per cent loans and low doc loans were put on the financial menu. Gateway Credit Union has never offered such products. Yet many credit providers have promoted this all-you-can-eat smorgasbord to their detriment.

Lenders need to go back to school and re-learn their trade and borrowers should modify their behaviour and live within their means. A refresher course right now in Banking 101 is just what the doctor ordered. Less spicy loans and a return to bread-and-butter lending standards will provide a boost to everyone's fiscal health.

Posting Date: 16 February 2009

Importance of spending

The underlying message in the blogs I've written over the past year is this: Economics is a social science. It is the study of human nature as it applies to money. When the history of the Great Credit Crisis of 2008/09 is written, it will focus on the behaviour of people.

One of the idiosyncrasies of the human species which will come under the historian's microscope is a phenomenon called The Paradox of Thrift. This paradox was first articulated by John Maynard Keynes and describes the dilemma that we face when times are tight.

During a recession, we are encouraged to spend to keep the economy going. But our natural and understandable tendency is to save which triggers a cause and effect spiral to decreased economic activity. Here's how the slippery slope unfolds.

The ride to recession begins when we all start saving our money which reduces consumer spending. This, in turn, causes aggregate demand to fall resulting in a decline in total income. When income falls, people have less to save.

As counter-intuitive as it sounds, individual saving makes us collectively poor! This paradox of thrift represents a form of prisoner's dilemma since saving might appear to be beneficial at an individual level but it's actually detrimental to the population overall. One person's spending is another person's income!

We humans never seem to get the balance right. We spent too much in the good times and are spending too little in the bad times. We've rediscovered thrift at the worst possible time. Debt fuelled spending got us into this mess, but paying down that debt too quickly has made the situation worse.

That's why governments are encouraging people to borrow and spend again by lowering interest rates. The money supply is primarily driven by banks and other financial institutions extending credit.

But people have become debt averse which has contributed to the dramatic contraction in the money supply. As a result, the wheels on the bus go round and round as governments and central banks continue their efforts to resolve the paradox of thrift.

Posting Date: 18 May 2009

Islamic banking

We all have regrets and one of mine is not undertaking an optional unit of study in Islamic banking as part of my MBA. No society can claim a monopoly on wisdom and humanity. We would all benefit from a sharing of ideas across borders and cultures.

The credit crisis has shown that the West's capitalist system is not perfect. The $64 million question is: Can we learn anything from the East's Islamic system of banking? Over the past year, I have read a few articles suggesting we can and that's what I'd like to briefly explore this week.

While I'm no expert in Islamic banking, I know that the rules and conventions are different from Western finance. Islamic law (*Sharia*) prohibits usury – the charging or paying of interest (*Riba*). Since lending and investment products cannot be interest based, they are offered on a profit-and-loss sharing basis (*Mudharabah).*

Loans (*Murabaha*) involve the bank purchasing a commodity at market value and then selling it to the customer at a higher price with the difference being the bank's profit. Similarly, interest is not paid on deposit accounts (*Mudaraba*) but investors share in the profit of the bank.

Loans must be used to finance tangible assets (car, home, equipment, etc.) and cannot be used to fund the purchase of intangible assets (like subprime collateralised debt obligations). This requirement to back every transaction with real, physical assets has seen Islamic banks unhurt by subprime toxic assets.

Sharia law also prohibits investments in businesses that are unlawful in Islam (*haram*) such as alcohol, pork, gambling and pornography. The concept of "principled investing" extends to short selling which is also haram.

The popularity of Islamic banking has spread to the West with London the headquarters for the new Islamic Bank of Britain. Locally, the ANZ Bank will become involved in Sharia compliant Islamic banking in Pakistan as part of its bid for the Royal Bank of Scotland's Asian network. In addition, the National Australia Bank recently announced plans to trial Muslim-friendly loans.

Islamic finance is an ethical and equitable mode of community banking and, in this regard, not dissimilar to credit unions. Islamic banking is rooted in the principle of justice with financial transactions required to be fair and equitable to all parties.

Posting Date: 16 July 2009

Mid-life crisis for economists

In the sixteenth century Nicolaus Copernicus led astronomy out of its Dark Age with his sun-centred (heliocentric) theory of the universe. Just as Copernicus started a revolution in scientific thinking, a leading economist, Anatole Kaletsky, believes that it's time for a revolution in economic thought.

In a recent magazine article, Kaletsky argued that "…Economic forecasters cannot predict the future for the same reason that weather forecasters cannot predict the weather – the world economy is too complex and too susceptible to random shocks for precise numerical forecasts to have any real meaning".

Economists not only failed to spot the financial crisis, they cannot agree on how to solve it. As a result, the profession is under the spotlight. In the words of one commentator: "An entire field of experts dedicated to studying the behaviour of markets failed to anticipate what may prove to be the biggest economic collapse of our lifetime".

There's no doubt the past 18 months has been a humbling experience for economic forecasters. Their "macro" models churned out predictions of "micro" accuracy. People are now asking whether economists really know any more than the rest of us. Just as (some) bankers needed a financial bailout, there is a growing chorus of people calling for economists to receive an intellectual bailout.

In fairness, economics is not an exact science like mathematics – it's a human science. The central goal of science is to describe and predict. But as we all know, it's impossible to accurately predict human behaviour and therein lies the problem. The economy is the product of human action and economists have been unable to build models which reliably describe the reason and logic of humans.

As economists go back to the drawing board, perhaps economics should be reclassified as a branch of psychology. Modern day economics has been variously labelled a flawed science, a dismal science and the science of ignorance.

While there needs to be a major rethink of economic tools and techniques, it's unreasonable to expect economists to be fortune tellers. In the words of celebrated economist John Kenneth Galbraith, "There are two kinds of economists – those who don't know the future and those who don't know they don't know."

Posting Date: 4 August 2009

Economic alphabet soup

Even though economists can't accurately forecast, this hasn't stopped the economic Nostradamuses from trying to predict the shape of the world's growth trajectory. Having survived the worst financial crisis since the Great Depression, investors around the world are now being bombarded with commentary about the form the economic recovery will take.

It's clear that the economies of developed nations will bounce back at different rates. But what is unclear is whether the various economic upswings will be "U", "V" or "W" shaped. These alphabetical economic theories were developed by economists to explain how an economy responds during and after a recession.

A "V" shape reflects a strong and quick recovery with the economy growing as dramatically as it slumped. A "U" shaped recession involves a longer trough and is followed by a slower and more gradual uptrend. Finally, in a double-dip "W" the economy relapses into negative territory after a temporary recovery.

There's no doubt the Australian economy is bouncing back, but which alphabetical metaphor will best describe our recovery? Will it be a powerful and bullish V shaped upswing, a more subdued U shape or even a "Wecovery" where growth will return for a few quarters and then peter out once more? As always, opinions are divided.

Australia has experienced eight recessions since the Great Depression but each one is different. Consumers adjust their behaviour from recession-to-recession. Around 50 per cent of Australia's GDP comes from consumer spending. When economists talk about a recovery, they are referring to growth in GDP. Consumers, therefore, are a central point of any analysis.

If you've kept up with me so far, then the $64 million question is this: Will Australian households spend us out of this recession (even though we're not technically in a recession)? There has been much talk of "green shoots" but my sense is that Australians have entered a new period of austerity.

So, my humble opinion is that…pause for effect…the only way to truly know the shape of any recovery is when it's finished. Beyond that, I'll stick my neck out and say I'd like to believe we're in for a rapid V recovery, but a slower U recovery can't be ruled out.

How's that for an each-way bet! "G", I think I'm now qualified to join the society of economic forecasters!

Posting Date: 6 October 2009

Money supply

One of my biggest frustrations throughout the Global Financial Crisis (GFC) was the ill-informed commentary from some sections of the media. An example is the erroneous claim that governments around the world were printing stacks of paper currency – absolute rubbish!

As I explained in a previous post, governments increased the money supply through electronic means, not by increasing the amount of banknotes in circulation. The money supply of a country consists of tangible money (physical notes and coins) and intangible money (balances in bank accounts).

Physical currency accounts for a very small percentage of the money supply and it's getting smaller. The motorway I drive on each day is cashless, my salary is directly credited to my account and I pay bills electronically.

There is now simply less need for cash (fiat money) and one day banknotes may even become obsolete like the old barter system (commodity money). Today, money largely exists in electronic format (electronic money) as records in a database of a financial institution.

Banks and other financial institutions are electronic rivers of money which flows in and out on a tide of transactions. They are also the creators of the majority of new money. Printing money now means creating credit.

When a bank makes a loan to a customer and deposits the proceeds into a bank account, new credit money is created. Thus, money borrowed from a financial institution increases the money supply. But this new money also has a multiplier effect.

For example, Bill borrows $1,000 from his friendly credit union. He uses the money to buy his wife a new ring. The jeweller takes the $1,000 and uses it to pay for major repairs to her car. The car dealer, in turn, uses the money to help pay the wages of his mechanics and so it goes on and on.

It can be seen that the same $1,000 gets circulated throughout the economy. The higher the velocity of money, the stronger the economy since the same fixed unit of money flows freely throughout the system.

The next time that someone tells you the printing presses are working overtime churning out more currency, tell them the value of notes and coins manufactured by governments pales into insignificance compared to the money created out of thin air by financial institutions.

Posting Date: 22 March 2010

Poor investment decisions

Decision making is central to human activity. We are all decision makers in both our private and professional lives. Many of the decisions we make as individuals are simple and routine (what should I wear?). Other decisions are complex and not run-of-the-mill (how should I lead my life?).

Most people don't spend a lot of time thinking about how they make decisions but there is a science to making optimal choices and judgments. It's okay to base frivolous decisions on feelings and preferences (emotion) but important decisions should be informed by data and facts (logic).

The decisions that we make about money are important and economics (rational choice theory) is anchored to the notion that individuals act rationally and consider all available information in the decision making process. Yet, in reality, many of us behave irrationally as investors.

Investor biases can distort our thinking and cause us to make bad judgments. The field of behavioural finance has evolved to explain why people make financial decisions which are contrary to their own interests. Here's a sample of the self-destructive cognitive errors made by investors.

Confirmation Bias. This is a type of selective thinking where an investor seeks information/opinions which align with his/her views about an investment and ignores anything which contradicts this belief.

Hindsight Bias. This causes investors to claim that a past event (e.g., subprime crisis) was totally predictable, thereby implying their ability to time markets to always buy low and sell high resulting in an inflated view of their predictive skills leading to overconfidence.

Overconfidence Bias. Most investors have an overly optimistic assessment of their knowledge, particularly in bullish markets, believing that good market returns are directly attributable to their own personal skills while blaming external factors when returns decline.

Herding. Many investors simply follow the crowd and are led astray (as in the dot-com bubble) since they mould their thinking to the prevailing opinion and make the same investment choices as others on the basis that if it's good for others it must be good for them.

It can be seen that people are not hard-wired to be good investors as their emotions can overtake their ability to reason rationally. So the message is clear: When investing, do not underestimate the impact of psychology. Your personality does affect your investment decisions. So tread carefully when investing and beware of human behavioural flaws.

Posting Date: 12 July 2010

New production model

The traditional roles of consumers and producers are intersecting. Consumers are increasingly performing tasks historically undertaken by companies. The Internet is driving a new business model called peer production (i.e., collaboration among a large group of individuals). Before examining the dramatic impact of this rapidly evolving socio-economic model, let's begin with a brief history lesson.

A hundred years ago, merchants manufactured products and services with no input from the end consumer. Consumers had to accept whatever was available. The classic example was Henry Ford who offered his customers any colour Model T vehicle as long as it was black. Mass marketing went hand in hand with passive consumption and gave consumers little choice.

After World War II, mass marketing gave way to market segmentation and greater choice. Customers became part of the production process and were encouraged to use technology to do more of the work themselves. Thus, furniture makers persuaded us to assemble our own storage units, financial institutions encouraged us to use ATM's and petroleum companies trained us to pump our own petrol.

Technology is now empowering consumers to shape organisational processes and customise products to their specific needs. BMW now allows car buyers to order custom built vehicles. Adidas enables runners to design their own shoes. And a Sydney surfboard manufacturer offers surfers the ability to specify the size, shape and colour of their board.

But it's in the area of information-based goods where peer production is a real game changer. Today, "digital goods" are created freely via donated labour rather than through labour that's hired and controlled by corporations. Examples include Amazon's customers donating book reviews, Wikipedia's readers writing entries for free and YouTube's users sharing their videos at no cost.

Internet companies which rely heavily on peer production (i.e., volunteer labour) are able to operate with a small, paid workforce. The global classified ad site, Craigslist, is one of the most popular sites on the web yet has only 28 staff. Likewise, PlentyOfFish, one of the largest dating sites in the world, has just three employees. And Wikipedia has only five full-time employees even though it's 42 times bigger than *Encyclopaedia Britannica*.

MySpacers, YouTubers and Wiki-users are at the vanguard of a movement that's redefining how we do business. It's all explained in a book aptly titled, *Wikinomics: How Mass Collaboration Changes Everything*. For those organisations still wedded to the traditional top-down command and control structures, beware, your days are numbered.

The Internet is enabling people to give their time and knowledge to non-monetary and non-market activities. People power is upon us. I'm just waiting for the day when borrowers and investors can go online and design financial products and services with options and features tailored to their specific needs. Yep, it's a brave new world!

Posting Date: 25 October 2010

Beyond GDP measurement

French President, Nicolas Sarkozy, believes it's an inadequate reflection of our true well-being. Nobel prize-winning economist, Joseph Stiglitz, argues that it needs to include broader indicators of prosperity. Humanitarian, Professor Muhammad Yunus, contends it doesn't measure the things which are important to society.

A growing chorus of economists, sociologists and politicians is saying that GDP – Gross Domestic Product – is an imprecise measurement of economic performance. Even the UN agrees and has developed an alternative measure, the Human Development Index, which considers life expectancy and literacy as well as standards of living as determined by GDP.

GDP became the prime economic indicator during World War II to monitor war production and subsequently became a universal measure for economic welfare. But it has long been criticised because it does not measure improvements in the quality of our lives.

A country's GDP is the market value of goods and services that it produces in one year – its domestic production. Most goods and services are produced for sale, so the money spent buying these outputs can be used to measure production. This method of calculating GDP includes expenditure in three categories – personal consumption, business investment and government spending.

But GDP only recognises goods and services that pass through markets. Production that is not bought or sold (e.g., peer production) does not get counted. Such non-market activities include household production – tasks performed by homemakers within their households for which they are not paid through the marketplace.

If you knit a jumper, this "production" does not get counted in GDP since it's never sold. The same applies to child rearing which is unpaid production. Yet most would agree that family caretaking is of enormous value to society and should be included in GDP calculations.

Volunteer work in the community does not count as part of GDP because there is no payment. Money spent on cleaning up an oil spill is included in GDP but the environmental impact is not measured. The sale of a new home is included in GDP calculations whereas the sale of existing stock is not.

Another problem with GDP is the underground economy. Some production goes unreported in an attempt to avoid tax. Examples include the waitress who takes tips that she does not declare and the mechanic who offers to work for less if he is paid in cash.

My sense is that there's a growing disconnect between people's perceptions of their economic well-being and the official GDP performance statistics. That's not surprising when you consider, for example, the rising cost of health care. It's tough on families but boosts the GDP.

I could go on but I think the message is clear: The current GDP measurement has shortcomings. I think it's high time that economists searched for a new definition of economic well-being. Maybe we should follow the lead of the Kingdom of Bhutan which measures Gross National Happiness. The King of Bhutan understands that good leaders value and measure the intangible.

_____

Posting Date: 1 November 2010

A banker's worldview

Perceptions rule our lives and create our reality. They are the lenses through which we "see" the world. But we see only what we are conditioned to see and this limits our horizons. We don't see with our eyes but with our brains. If we want to change everything, we have to change our perception.

Just as the northern hemisphere's summer is our winter, financial institutions also see the world upside down to those on the outside looking in. When it comes to banking, the view differs depending on whether you are on the customer's side of the counter or the financial institution's side.

When you take out a loan, you ("the borrower") acquire a debt which is a liability you must repay. However, to the institution that advanced you the funds ("the lender"), your loan is an asset or investment on which it expects a return. The return comes in the form of the interest you pay on your loan which is an expense to you but income to your lender.

The same logic applies when you invest money with a financial institution. Your savings are an asset to you but a liability to your financial institution. As an investor, you lend money to a financial institution which, in turn, pays you interest on the funds it has borrowed from you.

What I have just described is *financial intermediation* which is a pervasive feature of all of the world's economies. Gateway Credit Union is in the business of financial intermediation. In simple terms, this means we act as an intermediary (go between) in moving money between investors and borrowers.

We pay interest to investors on the deposits they keep with us and we receive interest on the loans borrowers take out with us. The difference between the interest we receive on loans and the interest we pay on deposits is referred to as our margin or spread.

The size of this spread is a major determinant of the profit generated by a financial institution. With borrowers understandably wanting the lowest interest rate possible and savers naturally wanting the highest rate they can get, margins are constantly being squeezed.

Whether this is a good thing again depends on one's perspective. If you view margin squeeze through the eyes of a customer, it means more competitive rates. If, however, your view is through the eyes of a shareholder, it potentially means lower share prices.

Interest rate wars between financial institutions exacerbate the margin squeeze. All retail deposit price wars have winners and losers. In Gateway's case, our members are also our shareholders. We serve only one master, so it's a win-win for us. Which goes to prove that a not-for-profit business model does have its advantages.

Posting Date: 25 April 2011

The productivity paradox

Some topics are conversation killers and productivity falls into that category. Most people don't like to be told they have to work harder and/or be more efficient. However, improving productivity has become a major goal in virtually every organisation in the world.

Whether we like it or not, we are now part of a global economy and better productivity is the key to global competitiveness. Increased productivity lowers costs and allows firms to offer more competitive prices in the hope of capturing a greater market share.

Improving productivity is not just important for businesses – it's also linked to higher standards of living for us as citizens. Renowned Harvard Professor, Michael E. Porter, succinctly sums up the importance of productivity in his book, *The Competitive Advantage of Nations:*

> Productivity is the prime determinant in the long run of a nation's standard of living, for it is the root cause of per capita national income. High productivity not only supports high levels of income but allows citizens the option of choosing more leisure instead of longer working hours. It also creates the national income that is taxed to pay for public services which again boosts the standard of living.

What is productivity and does it mean that we have to work longer hours? Contrary to popular opinion, working longer does not necessarily lead to higher output. Studies have shown that longer hours can lead to worker fatigue which actually lowers productivity.

The good news is that workplace productivity can be increased by working smarter not harder. This requires workers to be more efficient. It requires organisations to do more, with less. It requires managers to motivate teams to pull together to achieve optimal output through continuous improvement.

Productivity is defined by economists as a measure of output from a production process, per unit of input. Rising productivity implies that either more output (goods and services) is produced with the same amount of inputs (resources) or less inputs are required to produce the same level of output.

Productivity measures vary from industry to industry. Generic examples include tonnes of grain per hectare, motor vehicles produced per worker per day and incoming calls answered per hour. Looking at the economy as a whole, a classic measure is GDP/per capita (or per capita income).

In Australia, we put in more hours at work than most other developed nations. But we're not the most productive nation in the world – that title belongs to France. The French know that winning is not about working harder – as they work fewer hours than we do – but smarter.

Improving Australia's long-term prosperity and living standards requires increased national productivity. But our ageing population threatens to diminish our workforce and therefore productivity. We, therefore, need policies to offset the negative effects of an ageing population and to deliver improved workforce participation.

For Gateway Credit Union, improved productivity is integral to our long-term sustainability. Every day, our competitors are extracting efficiencies to improve productivity to sharpen prices (i.e., interest rates). Australians are now far more interest rate sensitive and increasingly shop around for the best rate.

As I outlined in a recent blog post, investors want to be paid the highest rate possible on their deposits while borrowers want to be charged the lowest rate possible on their loans. Only through improved productivity can we continue to meet the mutually exclusive needs of borrowers and investors.

Posting Date: 5 September 2011

In defence of deficits

It's a sweeping generalisation to say that debt is inherently bad. Most households have some debt which is perfectly normal. Without debt, the majority of Australians would not be able to buy a home or purchase a car. We use "good debt" to invest in the things which create wealth and help us get ahead in life. However, we should avoid "bad debt", like impulse spending on credit cards, since this detracts from our finances.

Just as households go into debt to buy the things they can't swallow in one gulp, so do governments. Building essential public infrastructure like roads, airports, sewerage plants, hospitals and schools is very costly. The revenue that governments receive from taxation is often insufficient to cover the expenditure required to fund necessary infrastructure projects.

Governments can increase personal and business taxes to cover any shortfall. But raising taxes is politically unpopular, plus it leaves taxpayers with less disposable income. It follows that if we have less to spend on goods and services, businesses will suffer. If sales fall sufficiently, firms might even reduce their workforce. Those without jobs will, in turn, have reduced spending power and so a vicious cycle begins.

A preferred way for governments to raise money is to issue bonds. Bonds allow governments to borrow money today and pay it back in the future with interest. Some believe this is wrong as it leaves a debt for our children as future taxpayers. But if this debt is used to leave a better world for our kids to live in, is it such a bad thing?

The real problem is that it's often difficult to know – unless a government is issuing specific purpose bonds – whether the bonds will be used to fund productive investment or non-productive expenditure. Issuing bonds to improve a nation's transportation infrastructure which generates economic growth and leads to job creation is an example of "good" (productive) government debt. Infrastructure is the backbone of future economic growth.

Conversely, raising debt to pay for public welfare schemes is "bad" (unproductive) debt as it imposes a burden on the economy. Paying pensions and health care to an ageing population does not facilitate economic growth or higher tax revenues, but is an important and necessary social safety net provided by governments. One of the reasons that Greece is in a mess is because it has used debt to fund a benevolent welfare state where pensions are ridiculously generous, tax avoidance is endemic and prospects for economic growth are bleak.

Governments have been borrowing for centuries and this will not change. There are two measures of sovereign debt: *current budget deficit* and *national public debt*. When a government spends more than it collects in any one year, a budget deficit exists. The accumulation of deficits over many years creates the national public debt. A crisis typically emerges when both of these are out of control at the same time.

Increasing national public debt can be an effective way to deal with economic shocks such as recessions, financial crises and wars. During World War II, the national debt of the UK and US reached very high levels – up to 150 per cent of GDP, but that money was eventually paid back. Similarly, the GFC led to a dramatic increase in the public debt of many advanced economies which implemented huge Keynesian-style stimulus packages.

Many economists agree that the actual amount of national public debt is less important than the percentage of debt to GDP. Public debt as a percentage of GDP in OECD countries as a whole went from around 70 per cent throughout the 1990s to more than 90 per cent in 2009 and is now approaching 100 per cent of GDP.

On an individual basis, Japan's debt-to-GDP ratio is 197.5 per cent, Greece is 142.8 per cent, Ireland 96.7 per cent, France 82.4 per cent, UK 76.1 per cent and the USA 62.3 per cent. Australia is not heavily indebted (26.6 per cent) and in fact has the second lowest debt of any developed nation. In contrast, Greece, Ireland and Portugal are overloaded with debt and can't just keep borrowing and spending in an effort to prop up demand. As they are now discovering, at some point the piper has to be paid.

The continuing growth of public debt worries many people which is understandable. However, economies are credit-driven which means that nations and households invariably have to go into debt in order to grow. Used wisely and prudently, debt at both a household and sovereign level should not evoke feelings of gloom and doom.

Posting Date: 10 October 2011

Greece is the word

Many English words in common use today are derived directly from the Greek language. The English language is figuratively indebted to the Greeks. How ironic it is then that Greece is now literally indebted to much of the English speaking world. Using words whose etymology is from ancient Greece, we can describe what is happening in modern day Greece.

When the ancient Greeks invented the word *"crisis"* they had in mind a short period of acute stress. The current sovereign debt crisis has been dragging on for over a year and there's no end in sight. The problems facing Greece are *"colossal"* (from the Greek word colossus meaning giant human statue) and solving them will require a *"herculean"* effort (from the Greek mythic hero, Hercules, son of Zeus).

The Greek government is in *"chaos"* (meaning state of confusion, opposite of cosmos) and one cannot rule out the possibility of Greece's exit or expulsion from the Eurozone. In ancient Greek mythology, Europa was a maiden princess seduced by the king of the gods, Zeus. This saga, known as the Rape of Europa, mirrors the turbulent relationship between Greece and the rest of Europe.

Anti-Greek sentiment has spread throughout Europe with the Germans being particularly angry that they are being forced to pay for a nation they believe has over-indulged. For their part, the Greeks are unrepentant for living beyond their means (spending and borrowing too much) and have taken to the streets in anti-austerity protests and rolling mass strikes.

"Marathon" talks (another Greek word) among Euro leaders at the recent G20 meeting in Cannes failed to come up with an acceptable rescue plan. There have been three "comprehensive solutions" so far this year. To paraphrase The Economist magazine, European leaders have been using an "inadequate

financial slingshot" and not a "big bazooka" in trying to save the Euro.

Greek Prime Minister, George Papandreau, lobbed a diplomatic hand grenade into the G20 conference. He threatened to submit the European rescue deal to a referendum, but, in the face of huge opposition, withdrew the call to put it to a popular vote. Meanwhile, the European press is running stories about Greece's exit from the Euro and plans for printing the new drachma.

Greece is now virtually an economic corpse. Ireland has received a bailout. Portugal, Italy and Spain are also drowning in an ocean of unsustainable debt. The European sovereign debt crisis threatens global economic stability. The head of the Bank of England referred to it as "the most serious financial crisis at least since the 1930s, if not ever."

Australia is not immune from what is happening in Europe with the Reserve Bank of Australia warning last week that our economy could be dragged down by Europe's sovereign debt crisis. We are seeing signs of weaker household and business confidence and the crisis is expected to push up the cost of funding for banks and other financial institutions.

While many have tried over the past year or so to find a solution, no one can be given *"kudos"* (yet another Greek word) for solving this mess. Many are saying it is a failure of leadership. Aristotle believed that great leaders use *logos* (logic), *pathos* (emotions) and *ethos* (values) to communicate effectively and persuasively. Perhaps our modern day leaders require lessons in how to employ all three of Aristotle's rhetorical elements.

Posting Date: 14 November 2011

Plight of retirees

We live in a society where we have to mind our Ps and Qs. Many are now too timid to defend their viewpoints and ideas for fear of offending. Political correctness has stifled debate to the point where we are walking on eggshells and cannot honestly express how we feel. Censorship has become a restriction on freedom of speech.

British essayist, Professor Stefan Collini, believes that criticism without censorship is the most genuine form of respect. In *That's Offensive!: Criticism, Identity, Respect*, Collini argues that one of the most profound ways to show respect for other people is by treating them as capable of engaging in reasoned argument and thus as equals in intellect and humanity.

I'd like to take a leaf out of Collini's book and lead an open debate regarding whether we care enough about self-funded retirees. I've written on this subject before but it bears repeating. When interest rates rise, we lament the plight of borrowers who have to pay more. But when rates fall, we are silent about the decline in income suffered by investors.

Mortgage rates are a political hot potato, so mortgage holders receive considerable attention and sympathy when rates go up. A hike in the cost of mortgages sours feelings towards the government of the day. Retailers, builders and other interest groups add fuel to the fire by blaming the Reserve Bank of Australia for their woes. The media also goes into overdrive, whipping the mortgage belt into a frenzy as part of the interest rate blame game.

Contrast this anger with the calm which greets an easing in rates. The tabloid press does not campaign on behalf of self-funded retirees for better term deposit rates. No powerful lobby group complains about the drop in the standard of living for older Australians. And the government is not moved to encourage banks to pass through, in full, rate rises on deposits to ease the cost of living pressures on seniors.

Around 1.6 million Australians live off investments and interest income. As more baby boomers retire over the next decade, a greater portion of society will become self-funded retirees and will welcome higher rates. Self-funded retirees were hit hard by the Global Financial Crisis. This group saw their superannuation capital plummet in the stock market downturn, yet they receive little support from government.

Many older Australians have worked hard and saved prudently to achieve self-sufficiency in retirement. They are responsible citizens who are to be applauded for standing on their own two feet. They are not a burden on the social security system as they reside outside the community of aged-pensioners requiring government assistance.

The next time that interest rates fall, spare a thought for the hardship this creates for the senior members of our society. It's true that housing affordability and mortgage stress are real issues for younger Australians. But it's equally true that older Australians suffer in a low interest rate environment due to falling income streams.

Finally, it's important to remember that interest rates go down when times are tough and rise when the economy is going well. Who wants to continually live in tough economic conditions? Let the good times roll.

Posting Date: 20 February 2012

Markets driven by emotion

Life has taught me to never underestimate the power of human emotion. Emotions play an important role in our lives and exert an immeasurable influence on every decision we make. We must often decide in the face of uncertainty, not knowing whether our choices will lead to benefit or harm.

When it comes to financial decisions, economists erroneously claim that we humans are rational and unemotional decision makers. Psychologists, on the other hand, correctly contend that economists' models bear little relationship to actual human behaviour.

Ergo, the myth of the rational investor is just that. Bombarded with constantly changing data, investors often buy and sell on a hunch or gut feel. Those with nerves of steel may go out on a limb, taking unnecessary risks, while others blindly follow the herd believing that there is safety in numbers.

Renowned investor, Warren Buffett, said we must "be fearful when others are greedy and be greedy when others are fearful." Human emotion drives financial markets as much as economic fundamentals. Winning streaks can make us irrationally exuberant while losing streaks can make us overly risk averse.

The now infamous phrase "irrational exuberance" was coined by Alan Greenspan in 1996 to explain the unsustainable investor enthusiasm that drove up asset prices to levels that weren't supported by fundamentals. The term was later used by Robert J. Shiller, Professor of Economics at Yale University, in his 2000 book of the same name.

In *Irrational Exuberance,* Shiller stated that the emotional state of investors "is no doubt one of the most important factors causing the (then) bull market." In the second edition of *Irrational Exuberance,* published in 2005, Shiller predicted the real estate bubble which led to the subprime mortgage meltdown and ultimately the Global Financial Crisis (GFC).

Many of the ideas put forth in his book fall into the realm of behavioural economics (or behavioural finance). Behavioural economics combines psychology and economics to explain how people make decisions when they spend, invest, save and borrow money.

The reality is we don't always weigh facts objectively and are influenced by our own biases when making financial decisions. There's no doubt in my mind that one of the underlying causes of the GFC was greed. In the pursuit of financial gain, many lenders, borrowers and investors did not act rationally.

According to David Tuckett, a professor at University College London, the 2008 financial crisis showed that human emotion has a critical impact on financial markets. In *Minding the Markets: An Emotional Finance View of Financial Instability*, Professor Tuckett argues that contemporary economics, with its neat mathematical models, fatally underestimates the importance of emotions.

Tuckett's core argument is that the short-term focus which pervades today's financial markets promotes irrational thinking amongst investors. In an earlier post, *Short-term gain, long-term loss*, I also highlighted the dangers of short-termism, not just in financial markets, but in all areas of society.

Regrettably, short-termism remains a serious and growing problem. It's a common human trait to focus on short-term outcomes. We prefer to see results sooner rather than later as we crave quick fixes and instant gratification. But as the GFC has painfully shown, short-term thinking can be very costly.

It's incumbent on political and business leaders not to give up the fight in encouraging long-term thinking in a world driven by short-term results. Best practice in corporate governance requires organisations to manage for the long-term.

Posting Date: 17 September 2012

History of money

We all have our funny little ways. One of my idiosyncrasies is a desire to know the history of things. History is inescapable as the present will never be free of the influence of the past. Everywhere you look, you find examples of living history. From the inherited languages we speak, to the ancient traditions we follow, to the modern versions of bygone technology we use, history links the past to the present.

History is certainly not a "dead" subject. Indeed, it's said that history is the narrative of humankind. History helps explain our beliefs, our values and our behaviours. It tells us who we were so we know who we are. History tracks our growth and development as a society and provides answers to how people lived.

Until the seventh century BC, humankind lived without money. In the beginning, our ancestors bartered with each other, trading items like cattle and grain. But swapping items of practical value had limitations, so more useful commodities such as metals were introduced as a medium of exchange. Early coins were made from precious metals but they also had limitations and were replaced by paper currency.

As we all know, paper currencies are merely "tokens" in the form of colourful pieces of paper that represent value but which have no intrinsic value in and of themselves. We now understand that money is information (stored in computers and magnetic stripes) and that it can be created electronically with the click of a mouse.

Money has a long history and has developed over thousands of years. In *The History of Money*, anthropologist, Jack Weatherford, takes us on a journey back in time to when money was invented. In doing so, he provides an enlightening account of money's role – from cows to computers – in shaping human affairs.

Since Weatherford's book is written through the eyes of an anthropologist, it provides a colourful socio-economic account of the evolution of money. We learn that primitive man exchanged cowrie shells, the Aztecs traded cocoa beans and the Anatolian kingdom of Lydia invented coins almost 3000 years ago.

Coins dispensed with the need to weigh gold for every transaction and gave rise to a new market system. This, in turn, sparked a monetary revolution that underpinned classical Greek and Roman civilizations. The Renaissance proved another turning point and brought with it banks and paper money which opened the way for capitalism, overtaking feudalism.

Weatherford identifies the introduction of metallic coins as the first revolution in money. The second revolution was the development of paper money. Not surprisingly, he cites the rise of electronic money as the third revolution. It can be seen that the history of money is the story of the gradual movement away from the immediately useful toward the symbolically valuable.

What Weatherford does not mention is credit creation – the most powerful mechanism used today to make money out of nothing. Today, printing money typically means creating credit. Banks and other financial institutions are the creators of this credit money through their lending activities.

Some believe that the primary cause of the Global Financial Crisis was the deregulation of credit creation. This, it is argued, contributed to a dangerous fall in mortgage lending standards which led to a burgeoning growth in debt around the world and ultimately resulted in a global monetary meltdown.

Gold fundamentalists believe we should turn back the clock to a system where money is based on precious metal. However, in a world of rapidly developing technologies and innovative payment systems using smartphone applications and electronic wallets, money's destiny is to become digital and virtual. The history of money is certainly not the future of money.

Posting Date: 8 October 2012

Future of money

In the beginning, we bartered for the things that we wanted. But swapping possessions of differing value was cumbersome, so metal coins with a specific face value were minted to pay for goods and services. Coinage, in turn, proved unwieldy because of the sheer weight of the metal needed to settle large commercial transactions, so light-weight paper currency was brought into circulation.

Cheques were later introduced to supplement banknotes as a medium of economic exchange with bank customers effectively issuing orders to their bank to pay money to a nominated payee. This led to the development of bank "clearing houses" which enabled the banks to exchange cheques with each other. Finally, credit cards gained mainstream acceptance as "plastic cash", thereby making credit money (consumer loans) available to the masses.

It can be seen that currency has taken many different forms and more changes are on the way. As cheques are being phased out and the utility of cash is decreasing, money is evolving again with the Internet unlocking new payment methods and virtual currencies. Money's destiny is to become digital which will give rise to the increasing use of electronic cash.

E-cash is money that is exchanged electronically. The transfer of money is done with the help of computer networks, the Internet and digital stored value systems. Specifically, money in your bank account is converted to a digital code, which is similar to a banknote number. This digital code may then be stored on, say, a smartphone which doubles as your digital wallet.

Apps are now available to turn smartphones into digital wallets. Waving a mobile phone near a cash register is faster than pulling out a piece of plastic or keying in a PIN. According to a recently released report by consulting firm, Deloitte, the practical distinction between real and virtual currencies is being rapidly eroded as people become more comfortable with e-cash.

"Consumers are making their purchases when and where they discover their need ... and often bypassing conventional payments solutions in the process," the firm's *The Future of Exchanging Value* report says. Deloitte argues that new payment models have the potential to disrupt current payment technologies and organisations and cites the following example:

> Early in the day, you arrive at the train station and join the queue at the coffee cart. Realising that you're in the queue, the vendor pings you via your smartphone and asks if you would like your regular order. By the time you reach the front of the queue your order is ready. You simply pick up your coffee, tap your phone against the vendor's terminal, and you're on your way to work.

Many would say the above scenario, using parallel networks for electronic cash outside of regulated channels, represents a threat to the traditional banking and monetary system. Electronic cash moves through a multitude of networks outside normal banking channels. The Deloitte report notes that "while the potential for disruption is high, the role of sovereign currencies and established payment solutions is secure in the short to mid-term".

There's no disputing the fact that a new generation of payment solutions has emerged. For example, PayPal burst on the scene in 1998 by providing an email-based web service to facilitate money transfers. In 2010, text message donations for the Haitian earthquake relief raised US$25m from 2.5 million mobile users in the US, according to Deloitte.

While I accept that physical cash is in serious decline and the popularity of electronic cash will undoubtedly rise, it will not spell the end of traditional banking or payment systems. Newer players like PayPal and Google Wallet, will certainly give established institutions a run for their money. Never, however, underestimate the ability of the banking sector to fight back.

When pressured to innovate or step aside, I have no doubt that banks and credit card companies (traditional transaction processors) will do the former.

Posting Date: 22 October 2012

Changing face of capital

During the first half of the 20th century, the key providers of capital were wealthy individuals with a single bottom-line agenda – to make money. Over the latter part of the 20th century, working class people, investing through their superannuation funds, provided private equity (capital).

A new form of capital is now available – crowdfunding. Crowdfunding is a way of raising money to fund an idea or business venture. A large number of people (the "crowd") are each invited to provide a small amount of money. The crowd is drawn from online communities.

Crowdfunding uses the Internet to reach thousands – if not millions – of potential funders. It makes use of the vast networks of friends, family and colleagues through social media websites like Facebook, LinkedIn and Twitter to get the word out about a new business and to attract investors.

Those seeking funds set up a profile of their project on a crowdfunding website. Arguably, the hottest crowdfunding site on the Internet is Kickstarter which was launched in April 2009. To date, the site has generated pledges of $700m from four million people to fund more than 45,000 projects.

There are four basic crowdfunding models.

- **Donation:** Donors give money for a cause or event with no expectation of anything in return.
- **Reward:** The person or business trying to raise money offers a reward/gift to those who contribute.
- **Debt:** Money is borrowed from the crowd using peer-to-peer (P2P) lending, also called micro-financing.
- **Equity:** A business raises equity online from individual or institutional investors.

Crowdfunding has many supporters, including Barack Obama, who sees it as a "game changer" and a boon to fledgling start-ups seeking capital. "For the first time ordinary Americans will be able to go online and invest in entrepreneurs that they believe in," the President said.

Tapping friends and strangers to raise money is also gaining currency in Australia. Unlike the US where some projects are now being promoted to contributors as investments, crowdfunding is being used here to harness funds on either a donation or reward basis.

Therefore, if you have a great idea and your bank won't lend you $50,000 to fund your dream, you can ask 500 people to each donate $100 to help your project take flight. If your project fails to reach its target, the pledge amounts are cancelled.

Australia's corporate regulator, ASIC, has warned there is a high potential for fraud on crowdfunding websites. Scams have already occurred with donations not being used for the intended purpose and projects being misrepresented by unscrupulous promoters.

Proponents of crowdfunding claim that it brings "venture capitalism to the masses". Others see it as the "biggest democratisation of capital access in history". It's also been billed as a revolutionary force to finance start-up companies as it "shifts investment power from Wall Street to Main Street".

I think crowdfunding is a fabulous way to solicit donations for charitable organisations, disaster relief, philanthropic activities and community projects. I also don't subscribe to the view that it's a threat to traditional business financing.

Just as I don't believe that Bitcoins will replace fiat currency, I can't see crowdfunding replacing debt-based bank funding or private equity venture capital. Contrary to the Internet hype, crowdfunding is unlikely to seriously challenge the dominance of traditional lenders any time soon.

Posting Date: 7 October 2013

Money and Bitcoin's future

It's part of our everyday lives. We work hard to obtain it. We then save and spend it. People are held to ransom for it. We envy others who have it. It's often linked to our sense of well-being and self-worth. Money plays a dominant role in society and some believe that it's humanity's single greatest invention.

Certainly, the world as we know it would not function without money. Money has shaped human civilisation and we use it to fund elections, bankroll wars and finance infrastructure. Money is classically defined in terms of its three main functions – a medium of exchange, a unit of account and a store of value.

As a *medium of exchange*, money enables us to pay for the goods and services we need. We use it to buy and sell from one another. Without money, we would have to barter for everything. Imagine asking a restaurant to provide you with a meal in exchange for washing the dishes! Money as a medium of exchange brings standardisation, making economic activity simpler.

As a *unit of account*, money (in Australia) is measured in dollars and cents. Everything in our economy has a dollars and cents price. Our restaurant meal cost precisely $42.75 rather than, say, ten-and-a-bit apples. Money is a standard numerical unit of measurement which is divisible into smaller units without the loss of value. What's a fraction of an apple worth to someone?

As a *store of value*, money can be saved and spent at a later date. Holding money is a more effective way of storing value than, say, holding a banana which will rot. The value of money saved remains stable over time and can be retrieved at any time. Of course, inflation slowly erodes the purchasing power of money over time but a dollar stored always retains its face value of $1.

Throughout history, a wide variety of items have served as money. These include commodity money (barter system), paper money (fiat currency), credit money (bank loans) and electronic money (e-banking). Recently, we have seen the development of another form of money – cryptocurrency.

A cryptocurrency is based on a digital medium of exchange and the best known example is Bitcoin. As I explained in *Bitcoin digital currency*, Bitcoin began trading in 2009 and since that time numerous alternate cryptocurrencies have become available. Official money now has to compete with all sorts of unofficial virtual money.

Acceptance of unofficial money and quasi units of value like frequent flyer points is spreading globally. As these virtual currencies can by-pass banks and government regulations, they are surrounded by many questions. The most common is: Will cryptocurrencies like Bitcoin ever replace official, government issued fiat currency? For me, the short answer is "no".

Bitcoin is like a religion and its advocates are evangelical in their belief that it will change the world. They are trying to convert an army of Bitcoin agnostics to have faith in their newfangled currency. Personally, I don't believe that Bitcoin will establish a New World Order and that I will have to kneel at the altar of a digital demigod.

As an online token, Bitcoin has not achieved broad acceptance as a *medium of exchange* in the mainstream real economy. It also fails the *unit of account* test since items bought with Bitcoins are not priced in Bitcoins but converted from fiat currencies into digital money. Finally, the growing number of thefts from digital wallets calls into question the safety of Bitcoin as a *store of value*.

I accept that Bitcoin will achieve a marginal place in the financial system as a payment mechanism. Beyond that, I'm not ready to jump on the Bitcoin mania bandwagon. While pro-Bitcoin enthusiasts see cryptocurrency as a vision of the future, I wouldn't be writing off fiat money just yet. Money will remain a tool of nation states with Bitcoin as a bit player.

Posting Date: 10 February 2014

Financial alchemy

The online Merriam-Webster Dictionary defines alchemy as "a science that was used in the Middle Ages with the goal of changing ordinary metals into gold". Medieval alchemists believed they could transform something common (molten lead) into something precious (pure gold). Viewed through a financial lens, alchemy is about converting a lower value item into a higher value item.

But care must be exercised since attempting to turn trash into treasure caused the Global Financial Crisis (GFC). The Alchemists of Wall Street transmuted toxic subprime mortgages into junk mortgage-backed securities and sold them as gilt-edged, AAA-rated bonds. Put another way, investment "lead" was dressed up as fool's gold triggering the worst crisis since the Great Depression.

Notwithstanding the dubious quality of the bonds that were minted on Wall Street, financial alchemy does have a good side. Governments (or to be more precise, central banks) have the ability to create sums of money out of thin air. This "alchemy magic" is called quantitative easing (QE) and it can help prevent an economy from slipping into recession.

In the aftermath of the GFC, official interest rates in the US and UK were close to zero. Both nations, therefore, had effectively run out of ammunition to stimulate their economies. While they couldn't make money cheaper, they had the power to make it more plentiful. So they decided to directly inject more money into the economy via a non-traditional weapon – QE.

QE increases the money supply – not by literally printing more money – but by introducing liquidity into the economy electronically. This liquidity is deposited with banks in exchange for selling assets (bonds) for cash. The theory was that banks would use the additional funds to lend to customers in order to boost demand and improve a sagging economy.

The jury is still out as to whether QE has been a blessing or a curse. While QE has not worked economic wonders, the deployment of artificially created money into the bond market helped stimulate economic growth. On balance, I believe that QE has served the global economy well and proved that monetary stimulus has an important role to play in economic recovery.

Beyond QE, all financial institutions are modern day alchemists due to the wondrous generative capacity of credit. Nearly all money is borrowed into existence. When a bank makes a loan to a customer and deposits the proceeds into a bank account, new credit money is created. Thus, money borrowed from a financial institution increases the money supply.

The amount of money a bank can lend is affected by the cash reserve set by the local banking authority. Let's say the cash reserve (liquidity) requirement is 10 per cent of a bank's total deposits. This means the bank can lend $90 when it receives a $100 deposit. That $90 is used by the borrower to buy goods and the shopkeeper deposits the funds with his bank.

The second bank takes the $90, keeps 10 per cent and lends $81 to another person. That $81 goes back into the economy and eventually finds its way into the other person's account at a third bank. The third bank, in turn, holds back $8.10 and lends out $72.90. This goes on until there is nothing left to deposit and lend out.

If you do the math, you will find that the original $100 eventually amounts to $1,000 in credit money and this is how banks create money through their lending activities. It's called Fractional Reserve Banking and it assumes that only a small percentage of depositors will demand their money back at exactly the same time. The rest is put to work as loans to borrowers.

Well, now that I've told you the inside story of the magic behind banking, it's time for me to say "abracadabra" and disappear!

Posting Date: 10 March 2014

Performance measure pitfalls

Distinguished economists, statisticians and mathematicians often have their names associated with some economic theory, concept or tool. Some examples include Giffen goods, the Nash equilibrium, the Phillips curve and the Gini coefficient. Today, I would like to introduce you to another economic concept – Goodhart's law.

This "law" testifies that social or economic performance indicators lose their usefulness when adopted as policy targets. Put simply, when a measure becomes a target, it ceases to be a good measure. One reason for this is that people change their behaviour when they are aware of their targets. The average person is skilful enough to make targets work for them rather than against them.

Some examples include the train driver who sets off without his passengers to avoid being late, the teacher who channels her students towards easier subjects in the pursuit of better average grades or the hospital administrator who orders patients to stay in ambulances as waiting times are measured from when the patient comes through the door.

Setting performance metrics for one part of a system often leads to sub-optimal performance in the overall system. Thus, if police focus on reducing one crime measure (e.g., shoplifting), other crimes increase. As a result, the shoplifting rate becomes a useless measure of the overall crime rate.

Goodhart's law is also true in business. When you set up a metric by which employees are rewarded or punished, they will act to optimise that measure. The classic example here is the call centre manager who puts a time limit on customer inquiries to artificially meet his department's time-limit target. After one question, his operators tell customers they have to phone back to get a second question answered!

Organisations use metrics for a variety of laudable purposes but often make the mistake of developing too many measures. Metrics should also encourage behaviours that benefit the business as a whole. Enron is an example of an organisation that had (apparent) solid financial performance which masked corrupt organisational performance. Metrics should measure whether the right things are being done at the right time all the time.

Effective metrics will provide a business with the information and insight to make the right business decisions. The most powerful metrics are those that directly measure desired business outcomes. In my experience, the best metrics are often subjective measures rather than numeric values. Which is why I'm inclined to hire someone who I (subjectively) believe will be a good cultural fit rather than someone who has straight A's.

Imagine if financial institutions around the world had metrics that encouraged behaviours which benefited the organisation as a whole. Regrettably, many Wall Street executives were remunerated largely against numeric targets (like profitability) and this monetary stimulus contributed to the destructive behaviours that led to the Global Financial Crisis.

The cliché, *"Tell me how I'll be measured and I'll tell you how I'll behave",* accurately describes human motivation. Financial institutions need to find ways to measure greed, ambition and ethics as traditional numeric targets encourage and amplify unhealthy behaviours.

Posting Date: 28 April 2014

Morality of money lending

Moneylenders have always had an image problem. In Biblical times, usury was viewed as an inherently evil activity and Thomas Aquinas condemned it. Dante Alighieri relegated moneylenders to the seventh circle of Hell with blasphemers and perverts in his epic poem, *Inferno*. Martin Luther and John Calvin both opposed lending money at interest.

Regrettably, there have been disreputable lending practices since antiquity. But moneylenders are not the villains behind every economic problem that humanity has ever faced. Yet, from the time of Aristotle – who believed the practice of money lending to be unnatural and unjust – credit providers have been loathed and derided by philosophers and theologians.

In the Bible, moneychangers are labelled as "thieves and marauders" and told sternly they were "wrong in what you are doing." Even playwrights have taken aim at financiers. In *The Merchant of Venice*, Shakespeare focussed on the relationship between a borrower and a lender in exploring the themes of money, debt and justice.

In more recent times, moneylenders have been blamed and castigated by everyone for causing the Global Financial Crisis (GFC). Irresponsible mortgage lending coupled with reckless financial engineering is seen as the prime culprit behind the global meltdown. In simple terms, junk mortgages were used to back triple-A rated securities.

Such poor and inexcusable lending and funding practices exposed the dark underbelly of capitalism. However, to blame credit providers alone is unfair. It's long been my contention that the GFC was also a cultural crisis. Our modern world is very materialistic and the demand for credit to finance our contemporary lifestyles is ubiquitous.

We as a society need to take a hard look at ourselves and ask whether we have become credit junkies. We need to understand that debt is not risk free and that we need to save more and encourage habits of thrift among our children. We can't play the victim and say "it's not my fault" when we overcommit ourselves financially.

It's a sweeping generalisation to claim that all US subprime borrowers were innocent victims of predatory lending practices. The reality is that borrowers, bankers and brokers were united in a delusional belief that US house prices would never fall. They all acted irrationally in expecting house prices to always rise.

At the end of the day, the GFC was caused by greed which manifested itself in financially reckless behaviour by both Wall Street and Main Street. However, while Main Street can be forgiven for its "irrational exuberance", Wall Street should have known better. The destructive policies of Wall Street and the shenanigans of some of the world's biggest banks were disgraceful.

I also acknowledge that in the aftermath of the crisis, Main Street felt abandoned while Wall Street was rescued. On the surface, this does seem unfair but rescuing troubled institutions was the lesser of two evils. Governments could not allow their banking systems to crash since it would have caused incalculable damage.

Have we learned from the excesses of the GFC? Only time will tell. What is clear is that money-lending will remain the lifeblood of our economy. Economies are credit-driven which means that nations and households invariably have to go into debt in order to grow. The good news is that, unlike in Biblical times, it's not hard to find a prudent lender – like churches, they are everywhere!

Posting Date: 12 May 2014

Rethinking economics

We humans sit at the apex of the evolutionary tree, but this does not make us the smartest animals on Earth. In fact, I'd argue that evolution has not equipped *Homo sapiens* with truly rational minds.

However, contemporary economic theory is premised on the assumption that human beings are rational agents or *Homo economicus*. The harsh reality is that humans do not obey the efficient, orderly principles that are espoused by free-market thinkers.

When it comes to money, we often act irrationally which is why humans are the X factor in economic theory. For example, *Homo economicus* is not supposed to buy a house at a grossly inflated price and expect its value to keep rising.

But that's exactly what happened before the Global Financial Crisis in the US where consumers behaved like *Homo sillyus*. Which is why Yale University economist, Robert Shiller, believes that the ultimate cause of the financial crisis was the psychology of the real estate bubble.

In the 2005 edition of his book, *Irrational Exuberance*, Shiller predicted the housing bubble burst. In a later book, *The Subprime Solution: How Today's Global Financial Crisis Happened*, Shiller outlined how borrowers, bankers and brokers were united in the delusional belief that house prices never go south.

There are a number of reasons why economists missed the warning signs of the crisis but chief among them, in my view, is that neoclassical economic theory is unable to account for flawed human psychology. It is because economists have unrealistic expectations of rational behaviour.

With regard to the US housing surge, consumer optimism led to "bubble blindness" and all logic flew out the window. When the bubble burst, markets tanked, people panicked and emotions took over. Fear drove extreme and unpredictable behaviour.

Deep down, I suspect that most economists acknowledge the limitations of economic theory in explaining and predicting social behaviour. The financial crisis confirmed that humans are far too emotive for rational economic models to accurately predict our behaviour.

The human species was convinced that it faced financial Armageddon and this supposedly intelligent herd animal behaved like one of Pavlov's dogs – the market rings the bell and hysteria starts. The great panic was fuelled by apocalyptic reporting from the media which whipped us into a frenzy.

The white knuckle ride was made even more exciting by market rumours. Nothing like wagging tongues to propel gloom and doom! One can only wonder if we had acted more rationally, could we have avoided or mitigated the financial system spiral which occurred?

As the dust settles on this damaging saga, teachers of media and political studies are trying to make sense of what happened. Hopefully, economists will learn that markets are not populated by rational decision makers.

They might also learn that the really big events in world history, as outlined in the bestselling book, *The Black Swan: The Impact of the Highly Improbable,* are rare and unpredictable.

The author of *The Black Swan* argues that economists live in a fantasy world where they believe the future can be controlled by sophisticated mathematical models. The growing realisation that this is not the case has led to a call for changes in how economics is taught at universities.

The economics profession remains dominated by neoclassical thought – the belief that markets are driven by rational choices.

Many see this as a false paradigm which is why much of the foundation of modern economics needs to be rethought.

Among the movers and shakers for change is a group aptly called, Rethinking Economics. The group was formed in 2012 to "…rethink academic economics and economics teaching, and to create fresh economic narratives to enrich the predominant neoclassical narrative."

I wish them well in their endeavours.

Posting Date: 22 September 2014

03.

social

Social forces are changing our world and the lives of individuals. We are living longer, marrying later and having fewer children. This is because our values, beliefs and attitudes are constantly evolving and impacting the way we live, work and think. We now think differently about many things including health, education, the role of women and environmental issues. Changing demographic and social patterns are the focus of this chapter with discussion on older workers, population growth, income inequality, social media, political correctness and values and ethics.

Banned aid solution to poverty

Humans love to debate and argue their points. Some high profile debates I have covered in this blog include the population debate, the climate debate, the welfare debate and the privatisation debate. Recently, I came across another debate which, I must confess, I had been oblivious to – the aid to Africa debate.

The leading combatants in this debate are two academic heavyweights – Jeffrey Sachs, Professor of Sustainable Development at Columbia University and William Easterly, a Professor of Economics at New York University. Both of these thought leaders want to eradicate poverty in Africa but bitterly disagree on how to go about it.

The vitriol between Sachs and Easterly is palpable and they colour their criticism of the other's position with personal attacks. Their rival opinions are expressed in their respective books in which both mount persuasive arguments. Sachs is the author of *The End of Poverty* while Easterly is the writer of *The White Man's Burden*.

Sachs is pro-aid while Easterly does not believe in development aid. Sachs contends that rich countries should inject massive flows of aid into Africa. Easterly, on the other hand, asserts that the billions spent on African aid have produced meagre results.

After reading *The End of Poverty,* I came away with a nagging sense that the effectiveness of foreign aid has been exaggerated. This troubled me to the point of seeking out a third view. So I turned to a book by another international economist, Dr. Dambisa Moyo. Like Easterly, Moyo believes that aid does more bad than good.

What makes Moyo different from Sachs and Easterly is that – as a black African woman – finding a solution to Africa's woes is "a personal quest". Born and raised in Zambia and educated at Harvard and Oxford, she worked for the World Bank as a consultant and then moved to Goldman Sachs. With such credentials, it is difficult to ignore Moyo's views on Africa.

In *Dead Aid: Why Aid Is Not Working and How There Is a Better Way for Africa*, Moyo argues that aid has compounded Africa's problems. "Millions in Africa are poorer today because of aid; misery and poverty have not ended but have increased. Aid has been, and continues to be, an unmitigated political, economic, and humanitarian disaster."

Moyo cites political corruption as one of the reasons for aid's troubled history. "The list of corrupt practices in Africa is almost endless", writes Moyo. "But the point about corruption in Africa is not that it exists: the point is that aid is one of its greatest aides. … Foreign aid props up corrupt governments – providing them with freely usable cash."

Moyo proposes aid-free, market-based solutions to development. She encourages African countries to look to international bond markets to finance major public sector investments, to foreign direct investment to finance large scale private sector growth and to micro-financing for local entrepreneurial development.

Micro-financing aligns with my long-held view that lasting solutions to human problems only occur when we move from institutional help to self-help. This principle is encapsulated in the proverb – *Give a man a fish and he will eat for a day; teach a man to fish and he will eat for a lifetime.*

Gateway Credit Union is a supporter of the micro-financing initiatives in Cambodia. We are doing our part to break the vicious cycle of poverty and we're making a difference. Therefore, I know from first-hand experience that Moyo is on the right track. We're quietly getting on with the job of helping the Cambodians become self-sufficient.

Moyo also believes that aid should be undertaken with less fuss and fanfare. She is concerned that rock star campaigners, such as Bono, have dominated the public discussion of aid to the exclusion of Africans with experience and expertise. While celebrity shots with impoverished children make for great television, they don't actually solve the problem.

Posting Date: 11 July 2011

Global population ageing

The elderly population of the world is growing at its fastest rate ever. The number of people older than 60 years will pass the one billion mark within a decade, according to a UN Report. This figure is forecast to soar to two billion by 2050 or 22 per cent of the world's population.

In 2000, for the first time, there were more people over the age of 60 than children under five. By 2050, the older generation will be larger than the under-15 population. The classic demographic pyramid – a small number of senior citizens at the apex and a broad foundation of children – is inverting.

Population ageing is a worldwide demographic phenomenon that has resulted from changes in fertility and mortality. Younger people are having fewer children and older people are living longer. The combination of declining reproduction and rising longevity is potent.

The world is entering unchartered demographic waters as the grey tsunami sweeps the planet. It is a megatrend that will transform economies and societies in both developed and developing nations. Precisely estimating its impact is a complex and difficult task but painting a broad canvass is possible.

The dwindling working-age population will cause labour force participation rates to fall. To help mitigate the drop in the ratio of workers to retirees, people will have to extend their working lives beyond the traditional retirement age. Countries may even start competing for immigrants to bolster their workforces.

Savings patterns will likely change because consumption as a fraction of income varies with age. Households save for retirement during their working life and spend (dissave) during retirement. Population ageing will put downward pressure on private savings which may lead to reduced investment.

Saving is a key determinant of economic growth. Societies must save to provide funds for financing investments in offices, factories, transportation, energy, etc. Older people running down their savings could lead to a shortage of savings and this could seriously affect economic performance.

Ageing will also drive governments to adjust their fiscal choices. The rising demand for age-related spending will see more nursing homes and fewer schools. Financial institutions must also adjust as they face increased demand for products that assist in the management of retirement incomes.

Population ageing will be a defining feature of the economic landscape for decades, particularly in Asia. It is said that China will become old before it becomes rich due to its one child policy. The supply of young people into the workforce is diminishing which threatens China's economic future.

Arguably the most challenged nation demographically is Japan which has been dealing with both an ageing and a falling population. Japan has the world's highest life expectancy rate and one of the lowest birth rates. Japan is seen as the canary in the coal mine for assessing how population change affects growth.

Economists argue that the world is now entering what Japan first experienced back in the 1990s when it suffered a "lost decade" of economic stagnation from which it has not recovered. A contributing factor was a shrinking labour force. Japan is the world leader in this demographic trend.

Japan has been described as a slow-motion disaster with a shrinking pool of taxable citizens and ballooning social welfare costs for an increasing number of elderly. The burden of old age support has become the responsibility of the younger generation. There are a mere 2.8 workers supporting each retiree.

While Japan has not coped well with adding wrinkles, I'm optimistic that the rest of the world can do better. The good news is that ageing is a gradual process and its consequences are predictable. The challenge facing policymakers is to deal with issues promptly before they become acute problems.

Posting Date: 15 April 2013

Economics of human longevity

Human life expectancy increases decade by decade. Globally, the number of people aged 65 and over is growing at around twice the rate of the overall population. By 2050, old people will outnumber children on the planet.

The magic age of 100 is becoming a milestone to which many now realistically aspire. This begs the question: How long can humans conceivably live? As far as maximum lifespan goes, scientists suspect it's around 120 years.

That sort of longevity will create a "demographic agequake" the likes of which we have not seen before in human history. Population ageing has profound implications for many facets of human life some of which are covered in a recently released discussion paper.

In *Living Until 120: The Implications for Absolutely Everything*, Australian actuaries Barry Rafe and Melinda Howes argue that longevity risk is a potential "black swan" that needs to be comprehensively managed, especially as it relates to the financial viability of pension systems.

"Longevity improvements will be a slow burn issue for many FS (financial services) businesses… however the implications are extreme for funds with guaranteed pensions", the authors warn.

They go on to say that the financial services industry faces "significant and unpredictable change" and provide a stark warning for financial product providers, saying they could lose their positions in the market to potential usurpers like technology companies.

"It seems that as wealthy people disaggregate their assets away from major retail service providers they may be attracted to products 'made' by trusted brands like Google and Apple."

The prospect of a smaller labour force having to support an increasingly larger older population poses a major challenge for society. People have an expectation that after a lifetime of paying taxes they are entitled to a government funded pension and health care in retirement. In acknowledging the existence of this "entitlement culture", the authors provided some sobering statistics:

> Currently around two generations of people pay for the retirement benefits of one generation. In our lifetime there may well be two generations paying for two post-retired generations and then potentially two paying for three. There is an important intergenerational equity issue. This is a moral issue.

In grappling with changing demographics, governments will be forced to make some unpopular decisions. "The concept of retirement and a fixed retirement age could simply disappear. Healthy people will be expected to work longer."

As someone who always tries to see the glass as half-full, I don't view a longer working life as such a bad thing. Many people in their 60s and older have much to offer economically because of their experience and wisdom.

It's clear that many public policies will need to change in order to cope successfully with the projected ageing of the population. The traditional retirement age of 65 will increasingly not be viewed as the beginning of the end of life. Thanks to advances in medicine, we can look forward to many happy and healthy years of retirement – even if we retire later.

Posting Date: 28 May 2012

Valuing older workers

In 1967 The Beatles released their now iconic album, *Sgt. Pepper's Lonely Hearts Club Band*. The album included the hit song, *When I'm Sixty-Four*. The song's simple lyrics have a young man asking – to a catchy tune – if his girlfriend will still be with him when he gets older, when he is 64.

While *When I'm Sixty Four* is a vibrant ballad, it also evokes fear of abandonment. Its refrain, *Will you still need me, will you still feed me, when I'm sixty-four?*, could well be the anthem of today's older generation who fear rejection and discrimination in the workforce.

Society faces real demographic challenges from the grey tsunami which is sweeping the world. The proportion of younger people entering the workforce is declining while baby-boomers, the largest age cohort, have started leaving the workforce.

As the baby-boom generation retires in greater numbers, nations will suffer a skills shortage in many sectors and governments throughout the developed world are worried. One way to tackle this problem is to remove barriers to labour force participation for mature age workers.

In Australia, we are at a critical demographic turning point. The baby-boom generation – the 5.5 million people born between 1946 and 1965 – has begun to turn 65 years of age. Baby-boomers make up 36 per cent of our nation's workforce.

The pipeline of baby-boomers expected to retire over the next decade will create a real brain drain, particularly in the managerial and professional services ranks. This is why the government will increasingly urge older Australians to stay in the workforce – but are they truly welcome?

Mature-age Australians are fitter, healthier and more active than any previous generation. Yet there remains a view that you can't teach an old dog new tricks. While you can't overtly discriminate on the basis of age, the reality is that younger workers tend to come out on top in company recruitment drives.

Paradoxically, the Global Financial Crisis showed that younger "whiz-kids" benefited from the wisdom of more market weathered colleagues in understanding the idiosyncrasies of markets. Ergo, effectively transferring the knowledge and insights of baby-boomers to the emerging Generation X leaders won't happen overnight.

The whole ageing debate begs the question: what does "old" mean? Well, not surprisingly, it depends on who you ask. Research reveals that younger employees consider a colleague to be "old" between the ages of 50 and 59. In contrast, three-quarters of older employees defined an "old" worker as being over 65.

Regardless of where you draw the age line, there's no doubt that stereotypes exist about older workers. Sweeping generalisations such as inflexible, frail, incompetent and slow are often used unfairly. The reality is that mature age workers exhibit lower turnover rates, higher levels of engagement and are typically better at the three Rs – Reading, wRriting and aRithmetic.

The "school of hard knocks" provides invaluable lessons which can be passed on to others. This is one way in which older workers bring benefits to organisations and to society overall. One of the key drivers of economic growth is the workplace participation rate.

An increase in this metric contributes to economic growth and improved economic prosperity for all of us. Which is why the federal government's third Intergenerational Report underscored the need for an increase in our labour force participation rate, particularly with regard to workers over the age of 50.

At the end of the day, we need older workers. In my case, I'm capable of changing a ribbon on a Remington typewriter whereas my tech-savvy adult children can't match their dear "old" dad in that area. Nonetheless, I know I'll have to demonstrate other skills to keep me employed in the corporate world until I'm 64!

Posting Date: 22 April 2013

Ethical lending and investing

On 14 December 2012, a 20-year-old man armed with semiautomatic pistols and a semiautomatic rifle killed 26 people – including 20 children – in an attack at the Sandy Hook elementary school in Connecticut. As the world mourned the loss of innocent lives and public outrage grew, there was a groundswell of discussion about the ethics of investing in gun manufacturers.

This prompted US private equity firm, Cerberus Capital Management, to sell its interests in Bushmaster Firearms International (BFI). BFI manufacturers the Bushmaster assault rifle that was used in the school massacre. Other investors also took aim and decided to divest themselves of shares in rival firearm manufacturers including Smith & Wesson.

Investors alarmed by gun violence expressed their concern by bailing out of stocks that did not reflect their personal values. This is referred to as Socially Responsible Investing (SRI) and over the past decade it has risen in popularity. SRI considers both financial return and social good and requires people to invest with both their head and their heart.

Conscientious investors want to have a positive impact on the world by not investing in "bad" companies. Such companies do "objectionable" things like pollute the environment, exploit workers and kill animals. Enlightened investors look not only at a company's economic performance but also at its social and environmental behaviour.

Tobacco, alcohol and weapons can kill people and ruin lives. We also know that gambling and pornography are human vices that can be addictive and create social problems. Each of us has the capacity to screen out businesses and "sin" stocks we don't agree with morally. Proponents of SRI argue we can all invest in ways that are both ethical and profitable, thereby encouraging sustainable business practices.

At a pragmatic level, it comes down to individual choice. We can choose to bring a higher, altruistic calling to the investment table. Given the option, would you invest in a pharmaceutical company trying to develop drugs which will save lives? Or would you prefer to invest in a tobacco manufacturer making cigarettes which cause cancer?

Financial institutions are now also expected to play their part in helping create a sustainable world by investing ethically. Money deposited in a bank account is a form of investment. Banks use customer deposits to make other investments in the form of loans. In this way, financial institutions have an indirect impact on the environment through their lending decisions.

An increasing number of banks accept that money can no longer be simply viewed as a commodity to be invested with no ethical implications. Many have switched away from unsustainable investing and lending practices and have adopted the "Equator Principles". These principles were put in place by the International Finance Corporation in 2003 in conjunction with the World Bank.

The ten Equator Principles are a voluntary set of standards. They're designed to ensure that a bank makes an informed decision with regard to the potential social and environmental risks when financing large scale (over US$10m) infrastructure, mining and energy projects as well as projects in other sensitive sectors.

Westpac Banking Corporation was one of the original 10 banks globally to adopt the Equator Principles in 2003. In 2006, the ANZ Banking Group became a signatory followed by the National Australia Bank in 2007. Credit unions, as socially responsible co-operatives, have always been committed to sustainable development in the communities in which they operate.

It can be seen that how individuals and institutions invest matters. It's also clear that the moral suasion of investors can

improve the behaviour of companies. The power of one is alive
and well and you can make a difference.

Posting Date: 18 March 2013

We are not equal

Imagine if we held award ceremonies where no gold medals, blue ribbons or 1st place trophies were given out. Instead all award attendees were given an identical certificate of participation. With no recognition of exceptional performance everyone – in theory – would be equal.

In practice, however, talent and ability together with drive and determination create inequality. In any group of people there will be those who strive for excellence. As a nation, we quite rightly acknowledge and applaud our high achievers in sport, academia, business and the arts.

While high-achievers become role models for others to emulate, they also create income inequality. People who work harder and smarter tend to be rewarded more. This contributes to the ever expanding gap between the rich and poor and the resultant call from some for a more egalitarian society.

The general premise of egalitarianism is that people should be treated as equals on a range of dimensions such as race, religion, ethnicity, political affiliation and social status. In broad terms, egalitarians argue that no one should be treated as a second-class citizen and I absolutely subscribe to that view.

I do not, however, believe that in an open-market, capitalist economy we can or should have equal economic status. People deserve varying financial rewards for the jobs they do and the contribution they make to society.

Even if we somehow managed to redistribute wealth so that every adult in Australia had exactly the same amount of money, it would be fleeting. The smart, the strong and the devious would quickly acquire the wealth of the slow, the weak and the gullible.

Also, people would use their money in different ways. The prudent would save and invest their money while the irresponsible would squander it. Some might gamble theirs away as soon as they got it while others still might simply give it away for altruistic reasons.

In my role at Gateway Credit Union, I see on a daily basis the different attitudes that people have to money and wealth. Some people are driven to increase their wealth and material possessions and borrow to buy multiple properties. Others just borrow to purchase the family home and are content with achieving that goal.

Given our diverse mind-sets to money, the equal distribution of wealth is clearly an unattainable goal. Nonetheless, I believe that the widening gulf between workers and executives has become excessive. I find it hard to accept that any one individual is worth an annual salary of, say, $10 million.

Equally, I don't believe that sports stars and rock-'n'-roll artists are worth the millions they are paid. However, I accept that in a free-market economy based on supply and demand, captains of industry, the sporting elite and entertainment celebrities can command multi-million dollar incomes.

Excessive greed benefits no one, but trying to make all of us financially equal is a recipe for disaster. Capitalism, quite rightly, rewards productive achievement and provides the necessary incentive for entrepreneurs to take risks and innovate and this benefits society overall.

Posting Date: 9 May 2011

Money and human behaviour

Money is a central component of our lives and influences practically every decision that we make. We need money to pay for our basic needs (food, clothing and shelter) and to finance our non-essential wants (exotic holidays, luxury cars and designer goods).

We each have a unique relationship with money. To some it's a drug they can't get enough of. To others, it's merely a means to an end. We can be the master and control money or we can be the slave and let it control us. We can also choose to be a prudent saver or an excessive spender.

Money worries are a significant source of stress for many Australians. Arguments over finances are the primary cause of family discord. When debt piles up, people feel a sense of hopelessness. Concerns about paying the mortgage and feeding the kids fuel frustration and anger.

Believe it or not, money even causes stress for those who are wealthy. Millionaires also suffer from financial anxiety although their worries are different. More money is seen by some as more headaches and more to manage. The rich typically worry about maintaining their financial status.

Interestingly, many affluent people don't "feel" well-off. In fact, some claim they are poor since they suffer from psychological poverty. I vividly recall from my high school economics lessons that there are three types of poverty: absolute poverty, relative poverty and psychological poverty.

Absolute poverty (destitution) describes people who lack the basic necessities for survival and literally struggle to stay alive. Relative poverty (economic inequality) relates to people whose way of life and income is lower than the general standard of living in a nation.

Psychological poverty (self-pity mentality) afflicts people who live in abundance but complain that they are barely getting by. Such individuals are said to have a warped sense of perspective about their fortune and can be viewed as materially rich but joyfully poor.

There has always been a gulf between the rich and the poor. Over recent decades, the gap between the haves and have-nots in most developed nations has widened. The working class backlash over rising inequality fuelled many of the post-GFC riots around the world.

It's not impossible to climb from poverty to the top but that invariably requires a higher education. As I outlined in my post, *Education and national prosperity*, education is one of the most important investments that an individual can make. A tertiary qualification is regarded as the pathway to success.

A person's health is also strongly influenced by his/her wealth. The relationship between socio-economic status and health is well documented. People with lower income levels experience the highest rates of illness and death.

At the end of the day, money is a social phenomenon like the Internet and Facebook. Society as we know it would not function without money. Money can help you acquire many things but it can't buy happiness. However, as a former colleague used to say, it can certainly take the edge off misery!

Posting Date: 8 April 2013

Income inequality

The rich are getting richer and the poor are getting poorer. This is happening all over the world causing the gap between rich and poor to rise. Wealth disparity is seen by many as a growing social problem. The OECD believes that inequality is a top economic risk and its reports, *Growing Unequal* (2008) and *Divided We Stand* (2011) ignited debates which continue today.

The OECD estimates that between 1980 and 2008, 22 per cent of all growth in Australia's household income went to the richest one per cent of the population. Salary and wages are the largest component of income for most Australians and, therefore, the most important driver of income inequality. Inequality aside, some argue that Australians have never had it so good.

According to journalist, Greg Jericho, (who draws on a 2013 Credit Suisse World Wealth Report), Australians are the richest people in the world. Our median wealth of US$219,505 per adult means we sit comfortably ahead of Luxembourg on US$182,768. The US, with a median adult wealth of only US$44,911, doesn't even make the top 25 nations.

Oxfam International released a report in November 2013 titled, *Working for the few*, which contained some startling statistics:

- Almost half of the world's wealth is now owned by just one per cent of the population.
- The wealth of the one per cent richest people in the world amounts to $110 trillion. That's 65 times the total wealth of the bottom half of the world's population.
- The bottom half of the world's population owns the same as the richest 85 people in the world.
- Seven out of ten people live in countries where economic inequality has increased in the last 30 years.
- The richest one per cent increased their share of income in 24 out of 26 countries between 1980 and 2012.

The Oxfam report states: "Some economic inequality is essential to drive growth and progress, rewarding those with talent, hard earned skills, and the ambition to innovate and take entrepreneurial risks. However, the extreme levels of wealth concentration occurring today threaten to exclude hundreds of millions of people from realizing the benefits of their talents and hard work."

It's important to note that economic inequality isn't just about how much you earn – it's also about how much you have. Which is why wealth distribution and income inequality are two different concepts. Wealth distribution examines how the ownership of assets in a nation is shared among the populace while income inequality focuses exclusively on the income side of the equation.

Income inequality is the extent to which income is distributed unevenly in a country. The most commonly used measure of income inequality is the Gini coefficient which summarises the entire income distribution for a country into a single number between 0 and 100. The higher the number the more extreme the nation's wealth inequality.

It follows, therefore, that a Gini coefficient of 0 represents complete equality – every person in a given country has exactly the same amount of income. In contrast, a Gini coefficient of 100 represents total inequality – one person has 100 per cent of the income and the rest of society has absolutely none.

With a Gini rating of 45 per cent, the US – according to the CIA Worldfact Book – has the highest level of income inequality of any developed country in the world. Australia's income inequality is not as lopsided with a Gini rating of 30.3. Scandinavian countries have lower levels of income inequality as prosperity is more broadly distributed in these nations.

Sweden, the most equal country, scores a rating of just 23. At the other end of the scale, Lesotho, in southern Africa, has the highest Gini coefficient with a rating of 63.2 which means the very rich there take home a large share of the economic pie. The gap between the richest and the poorest is most pronounced in African nations.

My personal views about the growing gulf between rich and poor were clearly outlined in an earlier post titled, *We are not equal*. In that post, I condemned excessive greed on the one hand while explaining the folly of egalitarianism on the other.

Posting Date: 31 March 2014

A library without books

One of my favorite pastimes is roaming through bookstores. I'm a book lover and enjoy browsing the shelves and leafing through whatever catches my eye. I like the intimacy of smaller book shops, particularly those with floor-to-ceiling bookstands, but also appreciate larger stores with plenty of titles.

If technology has its way, strolling through bookstore aisles may become a thing of the past. With the advent of electronic books (eBooks) the days of ink-and-paper books are supposedly numbered. While our ancestors read from clay tablets, the next generation will apparently view texts and novels on a battery powered device called an e-reader.

Welcome to the age of digital information where a hand-held e-reader can literally store hundreds of books. The first e-reader on the market, the Amazon Kindle, arrived in Australia late last year. Its makers claim that it will revolutionise the way we read in the same way the iPod changed the way we listen to music.

Like all technological breakthroughs, e-readers come with pros and cons. On the upside, they are lightweight and portable and can fit snugly into a small bag. School kids will be able to carry one e-reader instead of a backpack full of text books. E-readers also provide privacy – no one knows what you're reading since there's no tell-tale book cover.

But on the other side of the coin, I can't imagine curling up on the lounge with an e-reader. Nor will I be able to get the author to autograph my e-book. Unlike hardcover books, e-readers may break if dropped and they need power which may not always be available. The look, feel and smell of a new book also provide an important tactile experience which e-readers can't replicate.

While the debate rages between e-reading evangelists and hardcover traditionalists, the jury is still out for me. I'm sure that gadget lovers will readily embrace the e-reader but I'm yet to be convinced it will overtake paper books. At the end of the day, books are symbols and many of us like to display great works on shelves in our homes and offices.

Despite predictions to the contrary, DVDs have not led to the demise of movie theatres, the Internet has not wiped out shopping malls, home banking has not eliminated bank branches and I can't envision e-readers totally replacing paper books. Many people will continue to read cover-to-cover rather than disc-to-disc. Personally, I'd much rather turn the page of a book than fine-tune the pixels on an e-reader.

Posting Date: 8 March 2010

The eBook revolution

One of my favourite pastimes is reading. There's nothing more relaxing than curling up with a good book. I never read science fiction and I don't read horror stories (with the exception of some annual reports!). My home bookcase is stacked with books ranging in subject from management to history and science to philosophy.

Every now and then I deliberately read a book by an author who has an opposing view to mine. Being exposed to new ideas or perspectives from leading writers expands your horizons and challenges your thinking. We see the world not as it is but how we have been conditioned to see it. So, it's exciting to see the world anew.

Oddly enough, I was not an avid reader as a child. I now find it difficult to walk past a bookstore without going in for a browse. Time does not allow me to devour as many books as I would like, but that does not stop me from buying them. At any one time, I have a small pile of books on the shelf waiting to be read.

If I were not so "old fashioned", I could store all of the books on my reading list on one e-reader. I explained how e-readers work in a blog I posted two years ago titled, *A library without books*. That post received a record number of comments and touched a chord with many of my readers. Therefore, I thought I would revisit the digital revolution which is reshaping the publishing industry.

In just a few short years, eBooks have gone from being a fringe product to the mainstay of the publishing industry. While I personally prefer turning the pages of a real book, I'm starting to reluctantly accept that they may go the way of vinyl records. In the not-too-distant future, we may be forced to read the works of Shakespeare on a Kindle!

Kindle is the name of Amazon's e-reader and it is transforming the way we read. The great publishing houses – like Macmillan, Penguin, HarperCollins and Random House – are fighting for survival against the online giant which is Amazon. Amazon wants to cut out the middleman i.e., traditional publishers, by publishing eBooks directly.

It's said that Amazon is doing to publishers what Apple did to record labels. By providing the market with bargain priced eBooks, Amazon has become the 800 pound gorilla in the digital book market. Since the marginal cost of selling an eBook is basically zero, it is pricing traditional booksellers and publishers out of the market.

Another technology titan, Apple, is also involved in reshaping the book market. Apple's iPad is battling for supremacy against Amazon's Kindle. Things got ugly recently with the US government accusing Apple and five publishers of colluding to fix the prices of eBooks. The alleged price-fixing was in response to Amazon's business practice of selling eBooks for just $9.99.

Everyone loves a good fight and the e-reader saga is turning into its own business thriller. Not since Gutenberg invented the printing press have we witnessed such disruption in the book market. The evolution of publishing from print to digital has already contributed to the demise of the major bricks-and-mortar bookseller, Borders, and more casualties are expected.

In moving us from the paper mill to the hard drive, Amazon (the world's largest Internet retailer) and Apple (the world's largest technology company), are shaking the book world to its spine. I still love printed books but sense that one day I will be mourning their passing. Perhaps it's time I turned on the Kindle my wife gave me for Christmas.

Posting Date: 7 May 2012

Nature knows best

By far the smartest "person" I know is Mother Nature. We humans can learn much from her. She's been giving lessons in design for billions of years, but only in recent times have we started "enrolling" in her classes. The early students have looked to Mother Nature for advice in solving many of the problems we are grappling with as she's already worked them out.

Using nature as a mentor, professionals from a range of fields are now studying biomimicry. Biomimicry is the art and science of emulating nature's best biological ideas and applying these solutions to product design, architecture, engineering and even community design. Analysing a forest floor to invent a better carpet tile is an example of biomimicry.

Velcro is probably the best known example of innovation inspired by nature. The product's inventor, George de Mestral, stumbled upon the idea by examining how burrs stuck to the hair of his dog. By mimicking the strong attachment forces of the burrs' small hooks, he was able to develop Velcro straps and fasteners.

Pioneering companies are now capturing the ingenuity of nature and adapting it to solve and overcome challenges. For instance, in designing its new Fastskin biometric swimsuit, Speedo copied the hydrodynamic efficiency of the skin on nature's fastest aquatic creature – the shark – to reduce the resistive drag on swimmers' bodies.

Similarly, Airbus observed how sea birds sense gust loads in the air with their beaks and adjust the shape of their wing feathers to suppress lift. As a result, Airbus installed probes on its A350 aircraft which detect gusts ahead of the wing and deploy moveable surfaces for more efficient flight.

Biomimicry is set to usher in a new wave of energy efficiency. Indeed, some believe that biomimicry holds the key to our planet's energy future. Possible next generation energy sources include wind-turbines inspired by bees, solar panels inspired by moth eyes and electricity generation inspired by ocean currents.

From building an efficient waste treatment plant modelled on the way human kidneys process waste to constructing a high-rise building that imitates a termite mound for passive air conditioning, copying ideas from nature for the way we make or do things is gathering pace. But unlocking nature's secrets is not always an easy task.

For some years scientists have been trying to synthetically manufacture spider silk. Spider silk is one of the strongest materials on Earth and is a whopping five times stronger by weight than steel. If we can decipher the architecture of silk fibres and replicate their properties, we will discover an exciting new material which will have applications from medicine to engineering.

Businesses are increasingly turning to nature with some amazing breakthroughs in design. The science of biomimicry now has some very creative practitioners, but it does not have to be a solo effort. Organisations such as Ask Nature.org can help with the task of finding a solution in nature to a given human problem.

In the coming decades, you will see more biomimicry as nature helps us do more with less by showing us how to tap a seemingly endless wellspring of solutions. For now, I'll leave the final word to Janine Benyus, author of *Biomimicry: Innovation Inspired by Nature.* "Biomimicry introduces an era based not on what we can extract from the natural world, but what we can learn from it."

Posting Date: 18 July 2011

Conscious capital

If you studied economics in the 70s and 80s you would have been introduced to the teachings of Professor Milton Friedman. Friedman was a great yet controversial economist who came up with some contentious ideas. One of his most infamous assertions was that a company has no social responsibility to the public or society.

According to Friedman's stockholder theory, a company's sole concern is to increase profits for itself and for its shareholders. For many years, that single-minded and relentless pursuit of profits drove self-centred corporate behaviour. Many firms gave scant attention to their employees, customers, the community and the environment.

Over time, an increasing number of businesses started to realise that they had a role to play in eliminating discrimination, avoiding pollution, helping the community and making life better for their workers. Firms felt obligated to give something back to those who made their success possible and this became known as Corporate Social Responsibility (CSR).

Over recent decades, CSR has gained widespread acceptance in the corporate world. CSR is now used to describe the way through which a business takes into account the financial, environmental and social impacts of the decisions and actions it takes (the so called triple-bottom-line approach to business).

While CSR has become well recognised, new concepts of social responsibility – such as the need to create "shared value" – are gaining legitimacy. The term "shared value" was coined by Harvard Professor, Michael Porter, and describes a new form of capitalism which brings business and society closer together.

Porter argues that businesses – not governments – are best placed to solve social problems, which is why shared value has become the new CSR for business. Companies are now expected to bring a value to the world, beyond just providing a good product or service. The new equation for business is: economic value + societal value = shared value.

Economic value can take the form of increased financial returns, better brand equity, greater market share and more loyal employees. Social value, on the other hand, can manifest itself in improved health, better education, safer communities and a cleaner environment. Through shared value, businesses can prosper while simultaneously alleviating social problems.

An example of shared value in action is the Adidas Group. As outlined in *Forbes Magazine*, Adidas has partnered with Nobel Laureate, Muhammad Yunus's micro-finance organisation, Grameen Bank, to manufacture a low-cost shoe for the poor in Bangladesh. The shoes are cheap and affordable for the poor and have the added bonus of protecting them from diseases.

In the financial services sector, the principles of shared value can be found in what is called values-based banking and a good example is New Resource Bank. Based in San Francisco, the bank works with businesses, non-profit organisations and individuals to produce environmental, social and financial returns.

The bank is dedicated to advancing sustainability and lends and invests where it will make the greatest positive impact. As a "conscious capitalist", the bank's CEO does not view money through the prism of its classic definition – a store of value and a medium of exchange. Rather, he sees money as "a store of your values and an agent of change".

Conscious capitalism is a natural fit with credit unions. As not-for-profit financial co-operatives, credit unions are not focussed on the pursuit of profits, but seek a higher purpose by putting people before profits. We've always done what's right – the rest of the business world is just trying to catch up with us!

Posting Date: 21 July 2014

Leadership challenge

There have been more books written about leadership than any other management topic. Yet there is no universally accepted definition of leadership. Leadership means different things to different people – no one can quite get a precise handle on it. And, of course, there's the age-old question: Are successful leaders born or made?

Clearly, leadership is not an exact science but it's applicable to all facets of life. All of us are leaders as parents, teachers, citizens, employees, etc.. One of the traits of leadership is the capacity to make things better and to influence outcomes. To this end, I believe that everyone should feel empowered to drive change and to improve what they do.

I have two fundamental beliefs about leadership. First, leadership is not a popularity contest. Effective and decisive leadership means making unpopular decisions at times. I've had to make a few here at Gateway Credit Union but people respect you in the end for making the right choice. Leadership is about getting results and every decision I make is based on what I genuinely believe is right for the business and our long-term success. My job requires me to champion and lead change and this sometimes takes people outside their comfort zones.

Second, leadership is about role modelling. As a leader, you must set an example and practise what you preach. You will never earn the respect of people if you say one thing and do another. Leaders have a primary role for developing, communicating and living the values and ethics that define an organisation or indeed a nation. My personal conduct as CEO establishes expectations and standards that shape the culture at Gateway.

Now that you know my thoughts on leadership, please allow me to share another observation with you – leadership is non-hierarchical. The focus of the leadership literature is invariably on those who reach the top of the tree and this has blinded us to the true nature of leadership. An organisational title, such as team leader or manager, may confer some hierarchical authority but it does not of itself make you a leader.

The core competency of leadership is character and this largely relates to honesty and integrity. Your character says more about your leadership qualities than a title ever will. Good leaders are also humble – they develop strong relationships, they help others succeed and they serve rather than rule. For this reason, I believe one of the best books on leadership is *Servant Leadership* by Robert Greenleaf.

Servant Leadership puts serving the greater needs of others as the primary goal of leadership. Servant leaders serve others by investing in their personal and professional development, which is why we have a heavy focus at Gateway on training and learning. Within a servant leadership framework, everyone is part of a team working to the same end.

You don't need to be a larger-than-life individual to be a leader. But you do have to be authentic and trustworthy and this is where many leaders fall short. The Global Financial Crisis discredited the leadership and management practices of many financial institutions around the world and the current Sovereign Debt Crisis has exposed a large deficit in political leadership.

Politicians and regulators, driven by the maxim – *never waste a good crisis* – have moved swiftly to bring in new rules and regulations to prevent further economic crises. But as I argued in a previous post, *Corporate governance and the credit crisis*, the real issue is one of leadership and that is a far more difficult problem to solve.

_____

Posting Date: 5 December 2011

Marrying finances

The statistics are sobering: One in three Australian marriages ends in divorce. Splitting assets after a relationship breakdown can be a long, winding and painful road. Carving up the family home, disentangling bank accounts and determining superannuation entitlements are all part of the financial separation.

In short, love hurts – just ask Paul McCartney. His parting of the ways with Heather Mills cost him $48.7m. The financial impact of a divorce for an average couple, in relative terms, can be even more devastating. Divorce often results in a marked fall in lifestyle as the assets of one household (a single financial entity) are divided into two.

Divorce is the most effective divestment strategy known to humanity. There's arguably no quicker or more brutal way to lose wealth. Not surprisingly, when mature couples tie the knot again, many choose not to merge their possessions. It's often a case of once bitten, twice shy as parties who have been burnt before live together but keep their finances separate.

To have and to hold clearly takes on a different meaning the second time around. The scars from a previous division of marital assets sometimes never heal. The understandable desire to protect oneself leads to precautions such as pre-nuptial agreements. Second time couples are a little older and a lot wiser and, therefore, more cautious.

Money is often a major source of friction in marriages and can bring out intense emotions. But for those who remarry, love's even more financially complicated. Older couples are more set in their ways and have boundaries around how far they're prepared to compromise. They also display a general wariness about combining finances driven by a desire not to muddy the waters.

For those who don't join finances, it's a case of "His" account, "Her" account, and not "Our" account. Saying "I do" to his-and-her banking is one of the many financial matters that should be discussed prior to walking down the aisle. Couples must also decide how household expenses are going to be divided. Further, there needs to be agreement as to who is going to pay the mortgage or rent.

On top of this, each partner will bring financial baggage into the relationship. You may have the complication of child support, existing debts and differing credit histories. Moreover, you may have divergent spending and savings habits and perhaps even dissimilar financial goals for the future.

Love can conquer many things but disagreements over money can create a rocky road for the best of relationships. There's no one right way to blend finances but avoiding an open and honest discussion about how finances will be managed is a recipe for disaster. Getting your financial household in order is a necessary prerequisite to living happily ever after.

Posting Date: 19 September 2011

The power of nice

Have you ever attempted to change lanes and another driver deliberately speeds up to block your path? Conversely, have you tried to merge and had a driver slow down and wave you in? The first driver's selfishness will make you grimace while the second driver's kindness will bring a smile to your face.

In all walks of life, seemingly trivial acts have a marked impact on those around us. Yet, in the hustle and bustle of everyday life, we sometimes forget the common courtesies like saying "please" and "thank you". Being nice to other people makes you a better person and it's also good for business.

At Gateway Credit Union, we understand that small courtesies can make a big difference. Kind gestures create satisfied members and result in repeat business and long-term sustainability. Our business etiquette is based on turning common sense into common practice because it's the little things that matter.

I always return telephone calls and honour commitments I make and have instilled these disciplines into the entire Gateway team. Respect for others starts at the top which is why I treat employees with respect so that they, in turn, will emulate this behaviour to members.

Of course, we are not the only organisation to work out that manners are the foundation stone in building relationships with employees, customers and other key stakeholders. All organisations intuitively know that bad manners can be deadly to their reputation and bottom line.

Over the recent holiday period, I read a book that proves a little kindness goes a long way. *The Power of Nice: How to Conquer the World with Kindness* debunks the myth that nice guys finish last. Co-authors Linda Kaplan Thaler and Robin Koval offer their success in the cut-throat world of advertising as evidence that nice gals can finish first.

Thaler and Koval believe that being nice has made their company one of America's fastest-growing advertising agencies. "Our success was won not with pitchforks and spears, but with flowers and chocolates. Our growth is the result not of fear and intimidation, but of smiles and compliments."

In our dog-eat-dog world, we are taught that the best way to succeed is to take as much as we can for ourselves. The authors, however, argue that life is not a zero-sum game. "There's no need to squabble over who gets the biggest piece of pie – we just have to bake a bigger pie."

The authors note that behaviour in the business world is often ruled by the law of the jungle. "But cooperation is as much a successful strategy for the boardroom as it is for hunting down prey", Thaler and Koval contend. They go on to write that "helping your opponent can be one of the most valuable things you can do for yourself".

Something I have long believed is that the workplace should be light-hearted. To this end, one of our corporate values at Gateway it to "have fun". The authors cite research on the beneficial effects of humour and reveal that "…workplace jokes and laughter help to stimulate employee creativity and improve communication and trust".

The book is packed with great examples of how being nice literally pays off. The authors challenge the mean-spirited "me or you" mentality, showing with real-life examples that "nice" companies have lower employee turnover, lower recruitment costs and higher productivity.

Being nice has helped propel The Kaplan Thaler Group to the top of its profession and is central to our success at Gateway. We know the golden rule in successfully dealing with people is to treat others as you want to be treated. With a sector-leading 95 per cent member satisfaction rating, "being nice" has certainly paid off for Gateway.

Posting Date: 6 February 2012

Social media

In my youth, I had a Malvern Star pushbike with chopper handlebars, banana seat and sissy bar shocks. Back in the 60s and 70s, virtually every Sydney suburb had a hamburger shop that was run by a Greek family while the Italians invariably owned the local fruit shop. Life was great, optimism filled the air, my favourite vinyl (LP) record was *Hot August Night* and I used a Kodak camera.

How times have changed. Kids now ride designer bikes, McDonalds virtually wiped out the corner fish and chip shop, Neil Diamond has passed retirement age, Kodak has gone broke and Generation Y walk around with MP3 players and iPods. To quote the lyrics of 60s singer-songwriter, Bob Dylan, *"The times they are a-changin"*. Nowhere is this change more pronounced than in social media.

Social media is a phrase that is being tossed around a lot these days. But like leadership, there is no one universally accepted definition of social media. The omnipresence of social media is undisputed and Australia leads the world for time spent each month on social media websites. Some businesses are using social media tools to engage with their customers and to "build buzz" in a connected world. So what is social media?

Whereas traditional print media (newspapers, magazines) and electronic media (TV & radio) are a one-way broadcast of information, social media is a two-way "conversation". The conversation occurs online and allows people to communicate, collaborate, debate and share ideas. Think of social media as a virtual coffee shop or pub where you "meet" friends for a chat.

Social media allows online communities to form quickly and people are increasingly seeking the companionship of others via these digital neighbourhoods. For example, Facebook has almost 700 million users. If Facebook were a country, it would occupy the third position after China and India in terms of population. One-third of Australians are Facebook members.

There are six broad categories of social media: blogs, podcasts, wikis, social networks (e.g., Facebook), content communities (e.g., YouTube) and Microblogging (e.g., Twitter). These social media tools are becoming part of the marketing toolbox of businesses. Gateway was an early adopter of blogs and podcasts which have enabled us to get more personal with members and to show a more human side to financial services.

Anyone who doubts the power of social media has only to remember the strikes and protests which spread around the world last year. Using Twitter, Facebook, YouTube and other communication platforms, protest organisers quickly mobilised "flash mobs" to engage in civil disobedience. The real-time nature of social media has revolutionised popular political dissent.

Another example is a social media campaign in the US called Bank Transfer Day. It was started by a Californian woman urging consumers to take their money out of big banks and put it into credit unions by 5 November 2011 – Bank Transfer Day. According to the Credit Union National Association, the Bank Transfer Day promotion resulted in 650,000 new credit union members and $4.5 billion in new savings accounts.

Australia's big banks may also have to brace themselves for a social media led exodus of customers. A website called One Big Switch is urging disgruntled bank customers to leave in search of a better deal. One Big Switch uses people power to force companies to lower their prices and claims that over 40,000 people have registered for its "Big Bank Switch Campaign."

The power of social media is undeniable and it's here to stay. Social media platforms are redefining human communication. We are using new tools for doing old things. The world has changed and you can't pedal a Malvern Star down the information super-highway.

Posting Date: 27 February 2012

Healthy retirement

A sound financial plan is essential to a happy retirement. But quality of life in retirement takes more than money. You must also focus on your cognitive and physical needs. These areas of your life are just as important as managing your finances.

I've never met a person who does not want to be physically active in retirement. After leaving the rat race of working life, retirees want to be well enough to pursue hobbies and interests. Yet many of us lead lifestyles which will sabotage that goal.

A healthy lifestyle today will help protect your financial well-being when you retire. Given the rising cost of health care, good health is one of the most important investments for a secure retirement. To achieve this, some rely on good genes and others good luck, whereas for the astute it's about good planning.

There's no shortage of experts out there who can offer health planning advice to make the most of your retirement years. Feel free to surf the web and garner some healthy living tips from the myriad online self-help sites. Alternatively, you can find some good books on health and retirement.

Recently, I read such a book, albeit you may be frightened by the title. *Maintain Your Brain: What you can do to improve your brain's health and avoid dementia*, reveals that lifestyle factors play a significant role in protecting your brain as you age.

According to the book's author, Dr Michael Valenzuela, dementia is set to overtake heart disease as the number one cause of death in Australia within 30 years. Yet the main forms of dementia affecting people today are not genetic.

The good news is that there are practical steps that you can take right now to help prevent dementia. The foundation stones of a brain-healthy lifestyle are physical exercise, mental stimulation and social interaction. The sooner you start incorporating these disciplines into your life the better.

"What is the point of retiring with a healthy superannuation package at age 65, say, if we'll have become demented within five years or so?", asks Dr. Valenzuela. He goes on to say that "an ounce of prevention is better than a pound of treatment".

His practical advice is based on years of first-hand research and experience. "Those older individuals who partake in activities with a social, physical and cognitive component tend to avoid dementia, compared to those involved in less complex or intense activity."

With regard to physical activity, the good doctor recommends a combination of aerobic exercise (sustained activity that raises your heart rate) and resistance exercise (exerting your muscles over a short intense period of time). Physical activity that raises the heart rate and increases the body's need for oxygen has been shown to reduce the risk of dementia.

Your brain also needs a variety of activities to exercise its different parts, so intellectual pursuits like reading, brain teasers and puzzles are encouraged. Interestingly, individuals with higher levels of lifetime mental activity (via tertiary education and/or occupational complexity) have a 46 per cent lower chance of developing dementia.

Finally, participating in social activities, having a large network of friends and therefore feeling less lonely have all been associated with a lower risk of developing dementia. "The art of socialising", writes Valenzuela, "requires a lot of thinking, planning, reacting, predicting, and so on... that is, cognition!".

Currently, there is no cure for dementia. However, the choices you make in midlife can help keep your brain healthy as you age. Therefore, adopt a brain healthy lifestyle and reduce your risk of dementia in later life.

Posting Date: 5 March 2012

Cost of unemployment

Many Australians watched last year's London riots from the safety of their lounge rooms. In contrast, my wife and I had a much closer view of the worst civil unrest to hit Britain in 25 years. We were actually in London when the mob violence and rampant looting swept through Britain. It was truly frightening watching rioters ransack shops and torch buildings.

Everyone has an opinion as to why the violence erupted. Some cite moral decay while others blame rank opportunism. I agree with those who believe the underlying reason was social and economic inequality. For my money, this root cause was succinctly captured by one of the British tabloid newspapers with the banner headline – "The underclass lashes out".

Poverty and unemployment, two classic socio-economic factors – are often associated with social unrest. To this end, the first riots started in the working-class North London suburb of Tottenham on August 6, 2011. Tottenham is a low-income neighbourhood with some of the highest unemployment levels in London.

Many of the looters and hooligans in Tottenham – and the other cities in Britain which saw an outbreak of violence – were below the age of 20. Britain suffers from high youth unemployment. I still have vivid images of gangs of teenage boys in black hoodies – some carrying cricket bats and wooden planks – facing off with riot police on the streets.

As a consequence of the Global Financial Crisis (GFC), unemployment has risen considerably in many countries. As I outlined in an earlier post, this has contributed to protests in Greece, revolts in Spain, strikes in Portugal, rebellions in North Africa, a revolution in Egypt and, of course, the riots in Britain.

Around the world, demonstrators have taken to the streets to voice their anger at what they see as financial and social inequality. Given the sovereign fiscal austerity measures in place in Europe, the ability of governments to provide for their people has been seriously compromised.

When there is high unemployment, the population collectively pays less in income taxes which leads to a diminished capacity of governments to provide public services and welfare payments. Greece is one country that finds itself in this vicious circle.

In Australia, unemployment is the major reason for poverty. People with low education and skills are more likely to be unemployed or to have low wages. Moreover, the rise in long-term unemployment among older people will likely lead to a growth in poverty among the aged in Australia.

Australia also has considerable hidden unemployment. The streets are flooded with out-of-work executives looking for jobs as well as other individuals who have simply given up looking. These people are not counted in the Australian Bureau of Statistics (ABS) headline unemployment figures that are published each month.

Then there are the under-employed. The ABS deems a person with only one hour of work a week as being employed. Yet many of these people would prefer to work more hours if they were available. The bottom line is that we have a much higher level of joblessness in Australia than is reported in the official statistics.

In Australia, as in all developed nations, rising unemployment is linked to social deprivation. The longer the unemployment, the deeper and more complicated the social and economic problems it causes including greater crime, more divorces, worsening health, increased homelessness and lower life expectancy.

It can be seen that society pays a high price for unemployment. Its impacts are not just felt at an individual or family level but across the population as a whole. The cost of unemployment to society is enormous which is why job creation initiatives (starting with slashing red tape and reducing bureaucracy) should be a priority of all governments.

Posting Date: 9 July 2012

Corporate wardrobe

Mark Twain wrote: "The finest clothing made is a person's skin but, of course, society demands something more than this". Which is why we all have a wardrobe full of clothes. Some of our outfits are an appropriate choice for work and others are not, but by whose standards?

When I started my banking career over three decades ago, the rule was to look conservative and business-like. You were expected to present yourself in a professional and polished manner. I was encouraged to stock my closet with crisp, long-sleeve white shirts. And dark colours, such as black and navy, were the classic shades for a business suit.

What now constitutes appropriate corporate attire is open to debate with image consultants offering differing views. Some believe that you must "dress for success" while others argue that "less is more". As for Generation Y, there are more of them in the workplace than ever before and they don't want to get a dressing down from bosses for not dressing up.

Traditionalists contend that the dress etiquette for business has plummeted, citing the almost-anything-goes attitude when it comes to the office ensemble. Their fundamental concern is that office workers who look like pizza delivery personnel lose their professional identity. What you wear, the argument goes, sets the mental stage for work and garners respect from coworkers.

Modernists, on the other hand, maintain that you don't need a pin-stripe suit to be taken seriously. They say it's an antiquated Victorian attitude to expect a man to start the day by tying a noose around his neck or for a woman to cover her bare legs with oppressive skin-coloured stockings. Allowing casual dress, they opine, provides a more relaxed atmosphere and produces happier employees who can express their individuality.

Putting aside these two schools of thought for a moment, what should not be lost in this debate is the critical need to meet customer expectations. A personal example will help here. My wife and I are big fans of our national carrier, Qantas. Whenever Bev and I travel overseas, our preference is to travel with the 'Flying Kangaroo'. One of the reasons for this is the impeccable presentation of the cabin crew in the aisles and the flight crew in the cockpit.

As part of our flight experience, we expect to see the pilots wearing stripes on their sleeves or on the epaulettes on their shoulders. And we expect the flight attendants to be in stylish, designer uniforms. This gives us a sense of comfort as passengers that we are in safe and professional hands. I can categorically assure you that we would not fly Qantas if it introduced a casual attire policy for its flight staff.

Interestingly, Virgin Australia, which has had a more relaxed attitude among its flight crew, recently announced it wants to put the glamour back into its business flights. Virgin is sending flight attendants to charm school to learn the finer points of etiquette and grooming. Paradoxically, Richard Branson gets hot under the collar at the mention of neckties and believes they "are uncomfortable and serve no useful purpose."

Personally, I believe that if you're in a back-office job away from the glare of the public spotlight, some relaxation of dress policy is acceptable. But if you're a front-line person, you're a visual representation of your company and should dress accordingly. Even if the company you represent is a more "hip" organisation, broader business conventions should not be ignored.

Facebook founder, Mark Zuckerberg, learned this lesson the hard way. He upset potential Facebook investors by dressing casually for a meeting. He was labelled "immature" for wearing a hoodie at an IPO (Initial Public Offering) roadshow presentation. The message here for all businesses is that you should never give the impression you are a slipshod organisation.

There's no doubt in my mind that dress standards have slipped – and not just in the corporate world. What people wear today to weddings, concerts and other outings is much more casual than in the past. The All England Club – which runs the annual Wimbledon tennis championships – recently issued a dress code to address falling sartorial standards among its members.

In our haste to reject traditional business decorum, let's not forget that you never get a second chance to make a first impression. Yes, I know you can't judge a book by its cover, but society is very visually based. A potential client's first impression of your organisation may be the deciding factor in doing business with you or going elsewhere. That's why I still have a wardrobe full of crisp white shirts!

Posting Date: 26 November 2012

Pragmatic innovation

Never in my entire life have I had a genuinely original idea and I don't expect to. Indisputable breakthrough thinking and/or truly revolutionary products are extremely rare. Most alleged new ideas, products and services are, in fact, evolutions of previous concepts.

Isaac Newton famously acknowledged this when he said: "If I have seen a little further it is by standing on the shoulders of giants". One of those giants was Galileo Galilei who, like his more contemporary scientific genius, Albert Einstein, shattered the foundations of our beliefs.

It is fairly easy to rearrange prevailing information and improve existing products. But how many of us can be creative to the point of changing the status quo and making others think and behave differently? The well of human ingenuity may be bottomless but, in my opinion, it produces few eureka moments.

Businesses are always being admonished to innovate or perish. While I accept that innovation is an essential ingredient to business success, most innovation cannot be classified as ground-breaking discovery. Rather, it is the product of incremental change. McDonalds did not invent take away food but perfected the process for delivering fast food through franchisees.

Similarly, the car I drive today has far more gadgets and gizmos than the first car I owned 35 years ago, yet they are fundamentally the same. Both have four doors, four wheels and run on petrol. Only Henry Ford can lay claim to inventing the first mass produced car – the Model T – which rolled off the assembly line in 1908. Today's modern cars are not brand new inventions but the result of continuous, small step improvements.

Even in my own industry, financial services, I cannot think of any radical, game-changing products over recent years. Yet again, most innovation in banking stems from process improvement and not breakthrough products. Innovation in financial services lies more in process and organisational change than in new product development. An example of this is the home loan.

Thirty years ago it took over a week for a bank to approve a home loan as the approval process was centralised in the head office. Over time, banks decentralised decision-making and empowered area offices to approve loans and this cut the approval time to about two days. Today, thanks to even more streamlined approval processes some credit providers approve loans within two hours.

What has changed over three decades is not the product *per se* but the efficiency of the processes used to deliver it. Innovation in financial services is driven by a culture of continuous improvement. Organisational culture, in turn, is established by the leader. Innovation, therefore, is a function of leadership which is why I have worked hard to create a culture of continuous improvement at Gateway Credit Union.

Every Gateway employee is empowered to drive change and improve what we do for our members. Deliberately, we do not have a formal innovation strategy or a dedicated innovation department. Innovation is a continuous change management process and everyone has a role to play. Employees throughout Gateway can develop fresh solutions and offer new insights into how we can better serve members.

This leads me to my final observation about innovation. I have long believed that the greatest innovation is the ability to provide first-class service. I have never met a CEO who says that service is not important. Yet how many organisations truly deliver outstanding service? Promising to provide great service is easy on paper but actually delivering on that pledge day-after-day is incredibly difficult and comes down to the quality of the workforce.

I'm fortunate to be surrounded by a great team at Gateway – they make me look good! They generate winning ideas and work diligently to transform our business processes into continuing innovation. I'm not hanging out for Gateway to come up with the next "big bang" idea in banking. Our success is built on pragmatic evolution rather than illusory revolution. We are reaching for the stars and doing so in small steps rather than giant leaps.

Posting Date: 29 April 2013

Workplace design

It seems the days of having your own desk are numbered. First, there was hot-desking, then there was office hotelling and now there is activity-based working. While these corporate buzz terms must sound like mumbo jumbo to the uninitiated, they all describe an underlying shift in office design to ditch the need to have a dedicated desk for every employee.

Hot-desking comes from the nautical practice of hot-bunking where sailors share a limited number of bunk beds in rotation, resulting in the bed being warm from the previous occupant. In the same vein, hot-desking is a work space sharing model where one workstation is shared between employees who use it at different times.

A similar model to hot-desking is office hotelling which is a reservation-based work space sharing arrangement. Hotelling enables desks to be reserved ahead of time whereas with hot-desking it's a case of grabbing whatever is available. Hotelling allows workers to hit the ground running while hot-deskers have to hotfoot it around the office to find a place to work.

As an extension of the "me" to "we" trend in office accommodation, we now have activity-based working (ABW). The aim of ABW is to improve team collaboration with an employee's seating based on the activity or project being worked on at the time. ABW eliminates hierarchical structures as all project team members sit together at identical workstations regardless of rank.

It's clear that for some employees, a desk is no longer a cosy home-away-from-home adorned with pictures of loved ones. Non-territorial office design is forcing people to be wandering nomads, searching the floor for a home. This begs the question: Is this form of musical chairs played with desks really all it's cracked up to be?

Well, as with all new initiatives, it depends who you ask. The arguments for having no allocated seating range from cost savings to better teamwork. On the other side of the coin, detractors say that having a different desk everyday lowers productivity and creates confusion. Personally, I think flexible working arrangements can work but only in certain organisations.

Companies with employees who have no significant attachment to being in-the-office are prime candidates for hot-desking. Such organisations include those with large, on-the-road sales forces and those with staff (e.g., external auditors and business consultants) who spend most of their time in the client's premises and do not require a permanent home base.

Beyond that, I am a Doubting Thomas. A former colleague works in a major bank which utilises hot-desking and she is not a fan. Her team rarely leave the office, so everyone needs a desk every day. The first come, first served seating policy has apparently led to some interesting behaviour. Employees now get in earlier to secure a desk for the day and then go off to the gym.

This reminds me of a phenomenon I witnessed in Europe which is called the German tactic. Holidaying Germans are famed for rising at the crack of dawn to secure their poolside sun-lounge by putting a towel on it and then heading off on a half-day sightseeing tour. In the same way, office workers "reserve" a desk by throwing a jacket and papers on it to mark out their territory.

My above-mentioned friend has an allocated locker to store her personal effects. Every morning she clears her locker, searches for a vacant workstation and then plugs-in her laptop. She then undertakes a daily ergonomic workspace setup which includes adjusting the chair height, altering the monitor angle, arranging desk items and optimising keyboard placement.

I'm told this daily ritual takes every worker in the department about 10-15 minutes. Everyone has been allocated a mobile phone as it's difficult for a fixed line to follow you around the office. And the colleagues you were liaising with yesterday at one end of the office are today scattered at the other end of the floor making communication difficult.

Needless to say, hot-desking is not on my priority list. I'm yet to be convinced that the pros of communal seating outweigh the cons. Indeed, forcing people to put their bum on a different seat everyday may give the entire organisation a pain in the ass! Humans like to have an anchor point and hot-desks offer cold comfort to those wanting a familiar place to call home.

Posting Date: 6 May 2013

Higher education

University degrees – Richard Branson is not a fan of them and Bill Gates and Steve Jobs both started one but neither finished. These three businessmen are all remarkable entrepreneurs who have unquestionably proven that real-world smarts can beat classroom theory.

Each saw academic life as a waste of time, preferring to learn through the University of Hard Knocks. Does that mean a university degree is unnecessary? Do these diploma-less entrepreneurs know something that we don't? Why are millionaire dropouts now being studied in university courses?

On a recent visit to Australia, Branson reignited the higher education debate by essentially telling Australian business students not to waste their money on a degree. Branson views postsecondary education as overrated and believes that universities can't teach someone how to be successful.

"As an entrepreneur", said Branson, "you just need to be able to add up, subtract and multiply. You should be able to do that by the time you're 15. What matters is you create products that people really want. You can always get someone else to add up the figures for you".

There is no doubt that Branson is a very clever businessman. People like Branson are successful with or without a degree. He has an in-built entrepreneurial spirit that is hard-wired into his DNA. His innate, never-say-die attitude cannot be taught in a classroom.

However, that does not mean I agree with Branson's attitude to higher learning. He would like to see universities turn out more graduates who become employers rather than employees. But not everyone wants or can be an entrepreneur. Branson is a truly unique individual and not the norm.

For the rest of us corporate types, a business degree is a prerequisite to getting a job. The accountants that Branson uses to add up his books would undoubtedly have university degrees in finance and accounting. The same holds true for the lawyers who represent and protect Branson's interests.

Branson is very good at starting up businesses and then handing them over to professional managers to run. It's London to a brick that these managers are degree qualified. That was certainly the case with Brett Godfrey, the former CEO of Virgin Blue Airlines, who holds a business degree.

I agree with Branson that more real life learning should occur at universities. Harvard Business School built its reputation on practical business training via case studies. I also believe that universities would benefit from having more professors who have actually started a business or worked in one as a CEO.

Due to technology, the way we work is changing and so is the structure of the labour market. We need more graduates – not less – to increase our economic productivity and enable us to compete in a globalised world. A nation's greatest resource is its human capital and I support a smart Australia.

To state the obvious, a paper qualification is absolutely no guarantee of success. But the days of the mailroom trainee making it to the CEO suite are gone. The more tools that you have to get you started, the better. A well-rounded education is an essential item in your career toolkit.

Around the world, university dropouts typically do significantly worse than those who complete their degrees. Tertiary education invariably leads to a higher paying career, more secure employment and a greater choice of jobs. A degree remains one of the best investments that money can buy.

Posting Date: 20 May 2013

Faster not better

Fancy a 60 second body massage? How about a five minute romantic dinner? What about a red wine that's been matured for a week? Some things in life just can't be rushed, yet we're in a daily race against time causing many of us to be overloaded and over-caffeinated.

Nature doesn't hurry the ripening of a tomato or the setting of the sun, so why do we humans think that speed is king? We constantly watch the clock trying to fit in more and more. We want everything to occur at the click of a mouse, but in the words of Gandhi, "there is more to life than increasing its speed".

Like the hare and the tortoise in Aesop's classic fable, we all intuitively know that being the fastest does not guarantee success. Yet our lives are more hectic than ever as we juggle multiple tasks. The challenge for each of us is to find ways to occasionally disconnect from our turbo-charged world.

Research shows that our best ideas come when we are relaxed and I know this to be true. Some of my blog topics have effortlessly come into my head while plodding up and down the pool. And the idea for this post came totally out of the blue while I was relaxing on my recent holiday aboard a cruise ship.

What struck me as a passenger on the ship is that service does not necessarily need to be fast to be good. The ship's restaurants did not rush diners with a get 'em in, feed 'em, get 'em out attitude. Rather, they provided prompt and unobtrusive service which enabled diners to savour the moment.

In contrast, many businesses have a tendency to reward speed even though a slower pace can win the race. In my experience, great service invariably beats fast service. Most customers would rather receive competent service than get rushed out the door – as long as they don't have to wait to be served!

When I reflected on the outstanding service my wife and I received while cruising, it had little to do with speed. For me, four things stood out with regard to the crew – they were truly attentive, they really listened, they made each passenger feel important and they had superior product knowledge.

Over and above this, the crew never made passengers wait for anything and this, I believe, is the key to their success. Customers the world over hate waiting and – if the wait or queue can't be eliminated – clever businesses give people something to occupy their time so the wait seems shorter.

For example, at some airports passengers are forced to go for a long walk while their baggage is unloaded. The baggage claim hall is deliberately located at the very end of the airport so that by the time the passengers arrive in the baggage claim area their bags are ready to be placed on the carousel.

If you surf the web, you will find references to the psychology of waiting and queuing theory. In a nutshell, this science posits that our perceptions of time are distorted by our emotions. As we all know, time seems to drag when we are bored but seemingly flies when we are having fun.

So, the message for all businesses is clear: Give customers something to do as unoccupied time feels longer than occupied time. Waiting times may be inescapable, but they can be made less painful. Queue management is no longer a nice-to-do activity – it's a strategic imperative.

Posting Date: 9 September 2013

Hurry up and slow down

Are you always rushing from one thing to the next? Does your to-do list run your life? Do you have a chronic feeling of being short of time? Is your body sending you signals that things are out of balance? Would you like more time to smell the roses? Do you yearn for a lazy Sunday?

For many people, life is chaotic. As a society, we're living on the edge of exhaustion. Life has become a never-ending busy season. The cult of speed is manifesting itself everywhere. We have speed dialling, speed walking, speed reading and even speed dating.

We're always in a rush as our modern way of living assumes that faster is better. The world has become stuck in fast-forward and according to Carl Honoré, author of *In Praise of Slow: How a Worldwide Movement is Challenging the Cult of Speed,* we need to slow down and rebel against a hectic lifestyle.

Honoré is a London-based Canadian – he's also a recovering "speedaholic". His personal wake-up call came when he began reading one-minute bedtime stories to his two-year-old son in order to save time. Honoré confesses that he was a "...Scrooge with a stopwatch, obsessed with saving every last scrap of time".

His book provides a self-deprecating account of his personal journey in search of a cure to slow down. After his "bedtime-story epiphany", he decided to investigate how to change his "full throttle" lifestyle and discovered the slow movement.

The slow movement does not seek to overthrow technology nor does it desire to travel back to some pre-industrial utopia. And it is certainly not about doing everything at a snail's pace. Rather, the slow philosophy asks us to strive for one thing – balance.

"The (slow) movement", writes Honoré, "is made up of people ... who want to live better in a fast-paced, modern world". Being slow means controlling the rhythms of your own life. "Be fast when it makes sense to be fast", advises Honoré, "and be slow when slowness is called for".

He warns that "turbo-capitalism offers a one-way ticket to burnout". He views the clock as "the operating system of modern capitalism" and the thing that makes everything else possible – meetings, deadlines, processes, schedules, transport and working shifts.

Long working hours and living in the fast lane inflicts a toll on family life. "With everyone coming and going, Post-it stickers on the fridge door are now the main form of communication in many homes," laments Honoré. Not even technology can buy more time. Indeed, he sees technology as "a false friend".

Well, I should s-l-o-w-l-y sign off for this week lest I be accused of suffering from hurry up sickness. I encourage you to savour *In Praise of Slow* – at your own pace, of course. Meanwhile, I'll try and speed up Gateway Credit Union's already fast website as I've just learned that Gen Yers are not happy if a webpage does not download in less than four seconds. Whatever happened to patience being a virtue?

Posting Date: 2 May 2011

Certainty of uncertainty

Predictions are rarely accurate. While people want to know what will happen in the future, the truth is that no one really knows. But that has not stopped "experts" in a range of fields offering bold yet incorrect pontifications. For example, the history of predicting business trends is a tale of misjudgments. Just look at the track record of foretelling the future of computing.

In 1943 Thomas Watson (IBM) declared "the world only needs five computers". In 1977 Ken Olson (Digital) proclaimed "there is no reason anyone would want a computer in their home". Not to be outdone in the I-got-it-terribly-wrong category, Bill Gates told us in 1983 that Microsoft "will never make a 32 bit operating system".

I've always had a healthy scepticism of crystal ball gazers and so was drawn like a magnet to a book by investigative journalist, Dan Gardner. *Future Babble: Why Expert Predictions Fail – and Why We Believe Them Anyway,* is a fast and informative tome which reveals the repeated and sometimes monumental failure of expert predictions in every field.

Gardner reveals that he's "..always been fascinated in the way that experts are held up as gurus and taken so terribly seriously and when their predictions fail, people just shrug and walk away." He argues that the average pundit is about as reliable as flipping a coin.

To support this view, Gardner draws on the work of Philip Tetlock, a professor of psychology at the University of California at Berkeley. Following extensive research, Tetlock discovered that experts' predictions were no more precise than random guesses. Tetlock concluded that "...experts are about as accurate as dart-throwing monkeys".

Gardner surveyed the history of predictions and found a legion of oracles who got it wrong. H.G. Wells famously declared that

World War I would be the "war to end all wars". Albert Einstein argued that "only the creation of a world government can prevent the impending self-destruction of mankind". Biologist Paul Ehrlich, declared in his 1968 book, *The Population Explosion,* that "the battle to feed all of humanity is over".

On the other side of the coin, soothsayers failed to predict events that did occur. No one foresaw the fall of the Berlin Wall. No one forecast the rise in fertility rates after World War II. No one envisaged the phenomenal rise in Internet usage. No one factored the 9/11 disaster into scenario planning. And very few economists predicted the Global Financial Crisis.

From the Y2K hysteria to the fervent belief that the Japanese economy would permanently overtake the American economy in the 1990s, history is littered with examples of seers who got it wrong. Yet, as Gardner notes, the general public continues to put great faith in experts who never lose their widespread appeal.

I'm with Gardner when he says that "the future will forever be shrouded in darkness". Expert predictions fail because the world is complicated, yet our flawed quest for certainty continues. Only fools or geniuses try to predict the future – and I'm neither! By the way, I'm still waiting on my flying car, robot maid, paperless office and personal jetpack.

Posting Date: 28 March 2011

Leave a legacy

Imagine waking up one morning and reading your own obituary. That's what happened to Swedish chemist, Alfred Nobel in 1888 following the death of his brother, Ludvig. A French newspaper erroneously ran an obituary for Alfred (in lieu of Ludvig) which called him "The merchant of death".

Alfred invented dynamite and his (premature) obituary bluntly stated: "Dr. Alfred Nobel, who became rich by finding ways to kill more people faster than ever before, died yesterday". Not wanting to go down in history with such a horrible epitaph, Alfred Nobel set about improving his public image.

Nobel decided to bequeath most of the vast fortune he made from inventing dynamite to posthumously institute what became known as the Nobel Prizes. These prizes are awarded annually for eminence in physics, chemistry, physiology or medicine, literature and peace.

Alfred Nobel wanted to leave a positive legacy – as each of us can – and others have done. Mahatma Gandhi was an icon against oppression, Mother Teresa championed the plight of the poor, Sir Edmund Hillary was a legend in mountaineering and Margaret Thatcher is remembered as the Iron Lady.

What mark will you leave on the world? Will the world be a better place because you were here? What do you want your obituary to say? These are meaty and important questions. We can all ensure that our life counts by making conscious choices about the way we live our life.

Parents leave an important legacy as their children make a mark on future generations. Parents are leaders and the prime responsibility of any parent is to be an effective role model. Similarly, business and political leaders must also be effective role models if they are to leave a positive legacy.

Success in business leadership is not measured only in numbers. Great leaders leave an organisational legacy that transcends them and goes beyond fond memories. It is said that an executive's legacy is linked to his/her reputation for things like hard work, honesty and integrity.

While that is true, I believe there is one overarching characteristic of every great leader – emotional intelligence. In my career I've had the good fortune of working under many really bright and intelligent CEOs. While all were high in IQ, at least one was sadly lacking in EI – emotional intelligence.

Being smart in the classic sense does not mean you make good decisions. Leaders with low EI are more inclined to do things for personal gain as was the case with the former executives of Enron. Conversely, leaders with high EI invariably do what is best for the organisation and not themselves.

Without even necessarily knowing it, great leaders practise Servant Leadership, a concept I explained in a post in December 2011 titled *Leadership challenge*. Today, I reaffirm what I said back then i.e., good leaders are humble, they help others succeed and they serve rather than rule.

A great leadership legacy, therefore, revolves around the idea of selflessness. According to Jim Collins, author of the bestselling book, *Good to Great: Why Some Companies Make the Leap... and Others Don't,* "the best leaders blend extreme personal humility with intense professional will".

Collins posits that great corporate leaders are "self-effacing individuals" who are a study in duality – "modest and wilful, humble and fearless". The good-to-great leaders "never want to become larger-than-life-heroes" and are "seemingly ordinary people producing extraordinary results".

In short, a great leader is highly ambitious for the success of his/her company. He/She wants the organisation to succeed irrespective of his/her presence at the helm. The bottom-line message for all CEOs is that without a vision for the future greater than your own needs, your legacy will never be great.

Posting Date: 24 June 2013

Encore careers

When historians talk about turning points in history there is always debate about which events should be included. Major wars, natural disasters, scientific revolutions and social upheavals always feature in the list of decisive moments that have changed our world. However, single events – even the most dramatic – often prove less important in the long run in shaping history.

The true watersheds in human history often go unnoticed initially. Unlike the dropping of an atomic bomb or the landing of a man on the moon, major transformational changes occur subtly and their effects emerge slowly. Such is the case with the grey tsunami which is quietly sweeping the planet. The elderly population of the world is growing at its fastest rate ever.

I have written often about the far reaching effects of this demographic change. In my post, *The truth on population*, I reported that the proportion of Australians over 65 will grow to 25 per cent of the population by 2050. In a subsequent post, *Fear of demographic time bomb*, I explained how Australia's ageing population could lead to a fall in living standards.

More recently, in *Global population ageing*, I warned that the growth in people over 60 years of age is a megatrend that will transform economies and societies in both developed and developing nations. And in *Valuing older workers,* I foreshadowed that nations will likely suffer a skills shortage as the baby-boom generation retires in greater numbers over the next decade.

Just to prove that I'm not a total doom-and-gloom merchant when it comes to population ageing, this week I'd like to talk about a positive aspect of ageing – encore careers. The term "encore career" was coined by Marc Freedman and describes a growing trend among older people to undertake paid or volunteer work that has social impact.

The marked rise in life expectancy is causing baby-boomers to rethink how they will spend up to 30 plus years in retirement. A life of leisure might sound appealing but what about purpose and meaning? As I opined in *Work until you drop*, happiness in retirement is about being active and for many this will take the form of work.

It is predicted that older workers will look for new frontiers and many will seek endeavours that are different from their past experiences. Such "retirement" careers will enable boomers to put hard earned wisdom to work while pursuing fields and attaining positions that fulfil their passion. For some, this will be altruistic work while others will be remunerated.

A desire to give back to society and contribute to the greater good has seen some high-profile baby boomers adopt encore careers. Microsoft founder, Bill Gates, has embraced philanthropic activities. Former US Vice President Al Gore, has become an environmental activist. And 1950s and '60s actress, Brigitte Bardot, is an animal rights campaigner.

It appears that few baby boomers want to retire in the traditional sense i.e., stop everything and just sit at home waiting for death. Rather, they want to reinvent themselves by launching a second "career". These swan song careers will connect boomers to something larger than themselves as – after a life of full-time work – they have nothing more to prove.

Personally, I'm quite attracted to the idea of never retiring. When the corporate world tells me my time is up, the last thing I want is a sun-filled life of leisure. Rather, I hope to turn an interest into a gratifying encore career which fits around my life and not vice versa. Watching the grass grow or paint dry is certainly not for me!

Posting Date: 11 November 2013

Next please

We all have strengths and weaknesses. One of my faults is a lack of patience when it comes to waiting in line. If you want to really punish me, ask me to stand idly in a queue. I find waiting to be served dead boring – minutes seem like hours.

As it turns out, I'm not the only person who detests queues. Apparently, most of us become peeved when in a slow moving line. We feel a nagging sensation that our life is slipping away and become even more annoyed if another line is going faster than the one we are in.

Unfortunately, we can't escape queues since they are a ubiquitous reality of modern life. Every day, we routinely queue when waiting for a bus, purchasing groceries from a supermarket or buying a coffee. We are also put in a virtual queue when we phone a call centre.

Not even being on holidays provides relief from the need to get in line. Cumulatively, I have stood for days outside some of the world's most popular tourist attractions. Try joining the snaking queue at the Louvre in Paris – the prolonged wait would make the Mona Lisa frown!

Let's face it – standing in formation while facing the same direction is not fun. But some of the pain of queuing can be eliminated. Research reveals that the single greatest bugbear with queuing is a lack of fairness (i.e., people not being served on a first-come, first-served basis).

Almost nothing upsets the average person more – except perhaps a brazen queue jumper – than finding you have picked the wrong line. You watch in frustration as people who have joined another queue after you, get served before you.

Academics refer to this as a lack of social justice and it is easily overcome with single line queuing which ensures the principle of first in, first out (FIFO). Organisations typically use one of two FIFO systems – either "take a ticket" and wait to be called or join a "linear queue" and stand in line.

An exception to FIFO is priority queuing which gets you to the front of the line in return for paying a premium. Examples include business class airline passengers using express lanes and VIP amusement park guests joining a fast-pass line – a case of more bang for more bucks.

While single line queuing stops people jostling for position, it does not address the second biggest issue with queuing – boredom. According to the experts, boredom is the result of customers having too much "unoccupied time", thus the need to give them something to do.

The need to distract customers while they wait is the reason some restaurants give patrons a menu to peruse while in line. It's also the reason that some lift (elevator) lobbies are covered in glass. Building tenants can kill time looking at themselves and others in the mirror.

Supermarkets also understand the need to keep shoppers occupied and this is one of the reasons they have installed self-service checkouts. Apparently, this process actually takes longer than going through a normal checkout but feels quicker because the customer is doing something with their time.

When it comes to theme parks, Disney is considered the master at managing queues and customer waits. It has turned the art of crowd control into a science and has built an underground command centre to keep lines moving and guests entertained while waiting for rides.

With a little thought and planning, all organisations can improve queue flow. I look forward to the day when passport checks at airports can be made faster and more humanely. Until that time,

I'll just have to grin and bear it as governments have a monopoly on border control and shorter queues are clearly not a priority!

Posting Date: 25 November 2013

Money etiquette

Recently, I was listening to the radio while driving to work when an expert on etiquette was interviewed. She was asked to comment on correct behaviour in a range of social situations. Her dos and don'ts of modern life included: DO vacate your seat for an elderly person, DON'T use your mobile phone in a theatre, DO pay the bill gentlemen if you are on a first date and DON'T microwave stinky food in shared lunchrooms.

The interview prompted me to think about money and financial etiquette. In bygone days, it was considered impolite to talk about money in public. We now gloat about wealth and even celebrate the wealthiest Australians in a rich list published annually. Conspicuous consumption has replaced discreet saving and you would be forgiven for thinking that bragging about your finances is no longer a taboo subject.

Well, I'm not sure that's actually the case. Maybe I'm old fashioned, but my sense is that people still believe that money is a private matter. Crass displays of wealth (let me show you my new red Ferrari) and financial games of one-upmanship (my child goes to a more expensive private school than yours) are not considered good manners. For most people, money remains a personal and sensitive subject.

My professional life is based around borrowing and lending money. The rules I must follow in running a regulated financial institution are unambiguous. In our private lives, however, the rules of money etiquette are not as clear and this can lead to awkward situations. How much should I tip? When should my friend pay back the money she owes me? Is it fair to evenly split the bill when I've had a green leaf salad and you've had a 500g T-bone steak?

As with most areas of life, there are unspoken boundaries with regard to money. Asking a complete stranger how much he earns is clearly off-limits. Equally, telling the world how much you've just given to your favourite charity is also poor form. But declining to give money to someone else's pet charity in favour of your own preferred cause is quite acceptable.

What is right and wrong with regard to money manners is not carved in concrete, but common sense can go a long way. For example, we all know the difference between being generous and being flashy. But some things – such as re-gifting a present we don't want or need – are hotly debated. Those in favour of re-gifting argue it avoids waste while those opposed see it as passing along castoffs to an unsuspecting recipient.

Another grey area is weddings and deciding who should say "I do" to footing the bill. It's claimed that the cost of the average Australian wedding is around $40,000. It is a case of "here comes the bride and there goes the money"! Traditionally, the bride's family paid most of the wedding costs but now it is common for both sides to pitch in and share the expense. Common sense should prevail with contributions based on ability and willingness.

At the end of the day, conversations about money are fraught with danger, so tread carefully. Like religion and politics, we all have beliefs about money with the latter driven by our money personality type. Some of us are cautious savers while others are confident spenders. Regardless, most of us intuitively know the polite and proper ways to save and spend our money and are able to avoid financial *faux pas*.

Posting Date: 7 April 2014

Money disorders

You may not have heard of Adolf Merckle. The German billionaire committed suicide in 2009 by throwing himself under a speeding train. Prior to the Global Financial Crisis (GFC), he was ranked the 94th richest person in the world. Post GFC, Merckle lost over a billion dollars and although far from broke, he could not cope emotionally with the losses which he found "too great to bear".

We all have a relationship with money and for some that relationship is dysfunctional. If you let money rule your life, it can literally wreck your life. Even though we all intuitively know that money can't buy happiness, we often act as if it can. While no one wants to live in extreme poverty, extreme wealth on the other hand does not – in and of itself – make you content.

To be clear, having more money does not make us miserable but neither does it make us happier beyond a certain income level. As I pointed out in a recent post, *Income inequality*, Australians are rich by world standards. Yet, as a nation, many of us grizzle and grumble about our lot in life. It seems the more we have, the more we want.

Every day, marketers sow seeds of discontent in our lives by bombarding us with promotions about products and gadgets that are newer and better. Many of us crave the latest "must haves" and, as I opined in *Robbing Peter to pay Paul*, this puts us on a hedonistic treadmill, causing us to live beyond our means. In the worst cases, this can lead to spiralling household debt driven by excessive shopping and spending.

Compulsive buying is recognised as a mental disorder and this buying addiction afflicts both men and women. For compulsive shoppers, buying something creates a feeling similar to the euphoria induced by alcohol. Shopaholics are particularly attracted to online shopping as they can buy without being seen. But this pleasurable pastime can lead to financial disaster.

Another money-related additive behaviour is pathological gambling. This disorder drives people to play games of chance – betting on horses, wagering at cards and purchasing lottery tickets – to the point where it ceases to be a social or recreational activity. In Australia, 70 per cent of problem gambling is associated with poker machines and gamblers have a higher suicide rate than non-bettors.

At the other end of the scale are money hoarders for whom being frugal is an obsession. These penny-pinchers are reluctant to spend money, even on the essentials of life like food and clothing. They would rather shiver in a cold house than pay for the cost of turning on a heater. Money hoarders are over-savers who find it emotionally painful to part with their cash. Despite their "wealth" they live in the throes of poverty, robbing themselves of life's basic pleasures.

While money hoarders secretly squirrel away money, those who are guilty of financial infidelity hide their spending from their partner. They tell lies about their finances, like not revealing they have a credit card or that they have made purchases outside of an agreed household budget. Such people are said to be financially "cheating" on their spouse with their cloak-and-dagger transactions undermining trust in the relationship.

Even without financial infidelity, money woes are among the leading triggers of divorce. Climbing out from under a pile of bills can put a strain on any relationship and can see couples at each other's throats. Money is certainly the main source of stress for younger couples and families who see red when the household budget is in the red. And when tempers flare, people can say things which they later regret.

Money may make the world go around but it can also send us around the bend. Financially self-destructive behaviours are real and more common than we realise. If money is controlling your life, perhaps you would benefit from some professional advice. If you're into self-help, take care not to believe everything you read as you will come across many personal financial myths. So, look before you leap!

Posting Date: 14 April 2014

The super-rich

"The rich get richer and the poor get poorer", so the catchphrase goes. Well, according to Britain's *Sunday Times*, the super-rich are certainly getting richer. Despite the tough economic times, the number of billionaires living in Britain has more than tripled in the past decade.

Britain now has 104 billionaires with the elite members of this exclusive club sharing a combined fortune of £301bn. Britain has the most billionaires per head of population and London has become the super-rich capital of the world.

Seventy two of Britain's billionaires are based in London compared with 48 sterling-equivalent billionaires in Moscow, 43 in New York, 42 in San Francisco, 38 in Los Angeles and 34 in Hong Kong. London now accounts for almost 10 per cent of all the billionaires in the world.

The 2014 *Sunday Times* Rich List notes that nine of Britain's top ten richest billionaires were not originally from the UK. The richest Briton, the Duke of Westminster, is placed tenth on the list. Two Indian-born brothers top the list with a fortune of £11.9bn.

While London has clearly established itself as the hub of the international super-rich, other nations also boast ultra-wealthy individuals. According to *Forbes Magazine* Mexican telecom mogul, Carlos Slim, has a net worth of $72bn, Spanish retail executive, Amancio Ortega, comes in at $64bn while American stock investor, Warren Buffett, has amassed $58bn.

But the most fabulously wealthy individual on the planet is Microsoft founder, Bill Gates, with a net worth of $76bn. Gates has been named the world's richest man 15 out of the past 20 years. He recently regained the number one spot from Carlos Slim, who topped the *Forbes* rich list for the past four years.

As well as being back at the top of the billionaire's list, Gates has also been named as the person most likely to be the world's first trillionaire. Investment bank, Credit Suisse, believes that Gates, or one of the planet's other billionaires, could have a trillion US dollars to their name by 2039.

A trillion dollars can be expressed as a million million or $1,000,000,000,000 or 10 to the 12th power – and is roughly the GDP of South Korea or Mexico. Just to put this mind-boggling number into perspective, if you spent a million dollars a day, you wouldn't run out of $1 trillion for 2739 years.

About two-thirds of the 1645 billionaires on the *Forbes'* list built their own fortunes while 13 per cent inherited their wealth. The list of billionaires includes 172 women, 42 of whom appeared on the list for the first time in 2014. Retail heiress, Christy Walton, is the world's richest woman with a net worth of $36.7bn.

With the seemingly inexorable rise in the numbers of the world's super-rich, some believe that this elite group is becoming the dictators of 21st century. As I outlined in a recent blog, *Income equality*, the richest 85 individuals have as much wealth as half the global population – around 3.5 billion people.

Of course, the rich are not the root cause of poverty and in the case of Bill Gates and Warren Buffet, they have pledged to give away much of their wealth to charity. Around the world, many non-profit organisations owe much of their budgets to wealthy donors.

There is a growing call for the rich to be more philanthropic and the well-heeled are increasingly answering that call. A notable exception is Australia where our rich have traditionally been less inclined to support worthwhile causes.

There are signs, however, that a philanthropic culture is starting to take hold in Australia. May the joy of giving spread like wildfire as altruism makes for a healthier and happier society. In the words of Winston Churchill: "We make a living by what we get. We make a life by what we give."

Posting Date: 2 June 2014

Fun at work

Laughter is a defining characteristic of the human species. Children laugh around 300 times a day whereas adults laugh only 15-17 times. One of the reasons for this difference is the workplace. We spend a third of our waking hours at work and, sadly, many of us do not find it an enjoyable environment.

I have long recognised the contagious power of laughter and have never accepted that being in "corporate mode" means you have to wear a serious face. On the contrary, I actually encourage people to laugh, chuckle and joke. Consistent with this, one of our corporate values at Gateway Credit Union is to "have fun".

While I'm not Gateway's official court jester, I do my best each day to inject some infectious humour into the office. My PA, Marisa, bears the brunt of my corny jokes and antics. I play the comic since I know from personal experience that employees are much happier, less stressed and more productive in workplaces where humour is encouraged.

"Laughter above all is a social thing," says Dr Robert R. Provine, a behavioural neuroscientist at the University of Maryland and author of *Laughter: A Scientific Investigation*. Laughter is about relationships which is why "the requirement for laughter is another person", writes Provine.

Provine spent a decade studying laughter and is considered the world's leading scientific expert on the science of "Ha-Ha-Ha". He views laughter as a "vocal signal" which "almost disappears" when there is no audience. By studying "laugh episodes", Provine discovered that people who are by themselves are 30 times less likely to laugh than if they were in a social situation.

I didn't need to read Provine's book to know that laughter is one of the best ways to warm up a relationship. My wife tells everyone she married me because I made (and still make!) her laugh. Laughter creates a bond that brings people together. It also produces a positive emotional climate at home and in the workplace and there should be more of it.

Regrettably, many bosses believe it's unbecoming of a leader to be funny. Now that's a bad joke! As Provine notes: "John F. Kennedy was unusual among U.S. presidents in having both a presence of command and an excellent sense of humour." Good one, Mr President!

I have long believed that one of the great unsung leadership tools is a sense of humour. Stern-faced and tough-minded leaders don't necessarily get the best out of people. In my opinion, work does not need to be serious business. Good humour and high productivity are not mutually exclusive. Employers should see the lighter side of things and strive to make their organisation a great place to work.

This is more important than ever since we've just come through the worst financial crisis since the Great Depression. Many companies had to downsize and let go of good people. Those who retained their jobs are working harder and longer than before. Getting more out of less is now the mantra of many organisations and stress is at an all-time high for countless workers.

In the face of sobering economic shocks, it's still possible to make work fun – just ask search giant, Google. Its corporate headquarters in Silicon Valley California – called Googleplex – boasts unparalleled employee perks and benefits. These include a climbing wall, two swimming pools, seven fitness centres, eighteen cafeterias and multiple volleyball courts.

Google employees – called Googlers – love working for the company and many others would like to as well. Apparently, Google receives over one million job applications each year and hires only about 0.05 per cent of applicants. Wow!

While Gateway (unfortunately!) does not have the same facilities as Google, the credit union is nonetheless a fun place to work. Fun happens when there's mutual respect and open communication. This leads to high staff satisfaction and happy employees who provide better customer service – that's certainly been our experience at Gateway.

I'll leave the last word on this important topic to legendary inventor, Thomas Edison, who famously said: "I never did a day's work in my life – it was all fun."

Posting Date: 22 April 2014

Perils of short-term thinking

A few years ago I planted some hedges in my backyard. No matter how much I water and fertilise them, the hedges continue to grow at a pace largely determined by nature, not by me. The systems in nature can't be rushed, yet we humans think we know better when it comes to the systems we build.

Take the world of business – it's built on the notion of fast, faster, fastest. We want instant sales, instant profits and instant growth. We want it now and we're not prepared to wait. Investors and analysts demand quick returns and this drives corporations to manage to quarterly outcomes.

The constant pressure to deliver instant results has created a business cancer – *short-termism*. The effect of short-termism on capitalism is well documented. It has led to misplaced priorities which are not in the best interests of shareholders or society at large. What looks like success today can inhibit a company's competitive position tomorrow.

The dangers of short-term thinking were evident in the Global Financial Crisis. The manic pursuit of quick profits drove the speculative housing bubble in the US. Both borrowers and lenders saw real estate as a get-rich-quick scheme. Rampant short-termism drove the securitisation of mortgages that performed poorly in the long-term but generated lucrative fees in the short-term.

In a world of sound-bite journalism, the media fuels short-term thinking by lauding or disparaging companies based on the achievement of current earnings targets. Asset managers add to the problem by not providing better incentives to encourage long-term growth. And short-term investors, like hedge funds, perpetuate the here-and-now mentality.

Short-termism has become endemic in society. We want QUICK fix surgery to rectify imperfections. We crave crash diets to lose weight FAST. We consume energy drinks to heighten alertness NOW. We expect politicians to respond to tracking polls TODAY. And we demand that customer service and approval times be RAPID.

Some argue that our modern world has made us more impatient. In reality, our craving for quick fixes and instant gratification is biological. The short-term outlook of humans is hard-wired into the emotion side of our brains which focuses on immediate matters. Not surprisingly, this short-term genetic disposition is reflected in our institutions.

Politicians seldom plan beyond the current election cycle as the distant future is rarely on the electorate's radar. Therefore, the short-term need to win elections trumps the long-term need for policy reform including big decisions on infrastructure. Thus, Sydney's need for a second airport has been a political minefield for over 50 years – almost everyone supports it but no one wants it in their backyard!

One-airport cities make as much sense as one-horse towns. Yet Australia's largest and busiest city still has only one airport while New York has six, London has five, Paris has three and Tokyo has two. Sydney, quite rightly, calls itself a major global city but is notable among metropolises for having only one airport.

As a society, we don't plan adequately for the future since politicians align their agendas with short-term focussed voters. As I stated in a previous post, *Stop the pandering*, opinion polls and minority groups unduly influence policy formulation resulting in long-term economic credibility being sacrificed for short-term populist reforms.

To be sure, we get the politicians we deserve and, as I opined in *Democracy in danger*, we also get the media we deserve. As a society, we would rather read about the sordid private lives of celebrities than have a serious debate about the long-term benefits of public policy. As citizens, therefore, we are complicit with falling standards and the dangerous focus on the short-term.

Posting Date: 5 May 2014

Changes in work & service

My 60s childhood brought me into contact with a raft of people whose jobs no longer exist. It's been a very long time since I last saw an advertisement for a milkman, paper boy, petrol pump attendant, typewriter repairer, bus conductor, switchboard operator, toll collector or elevator operator. These jobs of yesteryear largely became obsolete due to technology.

In contrast, today's school leavers have an exciting array of occupations to consider including web designer, computer engineer, social media manager, Internet cafe attendant, biomass plant technician and molecular biologist. We already have self-driving trains and factories that almost need no human hands. In the future, we might have space pilots, robot mechanics, gene screeners, human organ developers and hydrogen fuel station managers.

Due to technology, nothing is forever anymore and the nature of work will continue to change. Yet work will remain central to our lives. Work provides us with an income to meet our material needs as well as giving us a sense of purpose and identity. Which is why we are invariably asked, "What do you do?" when we meet someone for the first time.

The shift to automation has reduced the nostalgic human touch. The service industry, in particular, is under fire for its heavy reliance on self-serve delivery systems. From banks encouraging us to use ATMs to petroleum companies forcing us to pump our own petrol, consumers are now part of the production process.

The key to success in this brave new world is for businesses to combine "high-tech" with "high-touch". In the financial services sector, we bank on technology (excuse the pun!) to provide customers with 24/7 access to their money. However, clever institutions combine Internet and online wizardry with personalised service to stand out from the crowd.

At Gateway Credit Union, we use high-tech processes to let members lodge a loan application over the web with little fuss or bother. But we follow up with a friendly call to acknowledge receipt of the application. While some companies use technology – like automated phone systems – to shield themselves from customer conversations, we actually encourage them.

This blog is another example of high-tech/high-touch and proves that social media is no longer just for teenagers. I use this blog to engage directly with members and potential members and to make a human connection. As an aside, my blog posts are uploaded weekly by my Online Content Manager – a job that did not exist a decade ago!

We live in a world where the Internet never closes and customers expect to find what they want online. With most websites offering faceless information, Gateway is trying to differentiate itself. Blogs add personality to a website and we want to use our online voice to engage and educate members and become recognised as a thought leader.

I acknowledge that many people lament the passing of "old fashioned" service. However, as a CEO, I understand why businesses have introduced efficient, quick and almost clinically streamlined service. The challenge for business is to automate with a personal touch and that's our goal at Gateway.

Our aim is to provide personal service in an impersonal world and this starts with me. In any organisation, the CEO sets the tone, articulates the service philosophy and demonstrates commitment to customers. In short, leaders must be examples of excellent service and I do this through a combination of high-tech and high-touch.

For those longing for a return to bygone days, do not despair. I believe it's still possible to have an interaction between two people that creates a meaningful experience. Customer service remains number one at Gateway and we have no intention of throwing out the baby with the technology bathwater.

Posting Date: 24 October 2011

Zero-sum folly

Ever watched two cars playing head-to-head chicken? The first to swerve loses the game. Let's suppose that neither driver chickens out and both stay on a straight-line course. They both "win" by crashing into each other.

Consider two swimmers who are ferocious competitors. One starts taking drugs and the other follows. The drug taking leads to an identical improvement in performance. Both "lose" since the end result is the same as when they were clean swimmers.

Another common win-lose scenario is parents fighting over custody of a child after divorce. Joint time previously enjoyed with the child must now be divided. The interests of the child are often overshadowed by parental bickering with the child as the "winning prize."

Let's up the ante and talk about warfare. Two superpowers are in an arms race. One develops a more destructive weapon and the other increases its arsenal accordingly. Yet, if both countries co-operated, they could avoid a military build-up by signing an arms limitation agreement so everyone wins.

I could go on but I think you get the gist of the win-lose mentality (zero-sum game) of humans. The tendency of people to focus on narrow self-interests in lieu of the best outcome for all parties led to the development of a branch of economics called game theory. This theory describes how the gain of one player is offset by the loss of another player, equalling the sum of zero.

The best known example of game theory is the Prisoner's Dilemma where two criminals are enticed by police to betray each other. The prisoner's dilemma – to confess or not to confess – underscores how our choices affect others and how the choices others make affect us.

The Global Financial Crisis (GFC) was a modern day prisoner's dilemma where the "every-man-for-himself" attitude saw markets crash as everyone tried to get to the exit door first. All the efficiencies of the free market flew out the window as institutions hid their bad loans causing credit markets to freeze as players did not trust each other.

A less dramatic economic example is interest rates. Post GFC, lower rates have become a zero-sum game for the economy as lower rates for borrowers (winners) translate into lower income for savers (losers). I believe that savers, not borrowers, have been the main victims of the GFC.

The notion that someone has to lose for someone else to gain is narrow-minded. We humans must learn to modify this self-defeating attitude as zero-sum assumptions inevitably lead to conflict. Which is why game theory should be a compulsory element of the core curriculum of educational institutions.

We should all be taught that by changing the frame of negotiations from win-lose to win-win, both sides can benefit by working together on mutual outcomes. It's called expanding the pie. A simple example taken from a book I read many years ago called, *Getting to Yes*, is very helpful.

The book advises parties entering negotiations to focus on interests and not positions. It gives an example of two men in a library arguing over the position of a window. One wants the window open while the other wants the window closed – a seemingly win-lose scenario.

The librarian intervenes and asks both men what their underlying interest is in having the window either open or closed. One wants fresh air (so an open window) and the other wants no draft (so a closed window). Thinking creatively, the librarian then fully opens a window in the next room thereby bringing in fresh air without a draft and both men are happy.

Win-win solutions abound and school children and management graduates alike should be taught the benefits of co-operation over conflict. This training should begin in the home. After all, parents are the world's first and foremost teachers. We can all play a part in making our planet a better place via collaborative decision making.

Posting Date: 9 June 2014

The happiness equation

Most scientific laws can be expressed in concise mathematical equations such as Einstein's $E=mc^2$. These equations underpin universal laws which describe how the physical universe functions in a predictable and repeatable way. The speed of light is constant. The planets circle the sun in stable orbits. Magnetic needles always point north. Energy is never lost.

Outside the realms of science, I am unaware of any "laws" which are absolute, definitive truths. Yet many self-appointed experts claim there are universal laws for success and achievement. These so-called laws or theories are based on words which, unlike numbers, cannot be precisely tested. Numbers and formulae distinguish true science from hocus-pocus.

When it comes to money, there's a gaggle of gurus who postulate some magic formula for building wealth. The harsh reality is there's no off-the-shelf, mathematical recipe for financial success. Unlike Newton's laws of motion or Einstein's theory of relativity, money management is not an exact science. In fact, it's a very personal thing which mirrors the way we live our lives.

Some people are defined by money and do everything within their power to increase their net worth. Others see money as merely a means to an end and seek a deeper form of wealth in life. Aiming to be the richest person on the block or the happiest is clearly an individual choice.

Regardless, you need a financial plan to turn your goals into reality – you just can't leave it to fate. You must have two hands firmly on the driver's wheel of life and steer in the direction you want. All of us must take responsibility for being in control of our lives.

The business maxim – *"If you fail to plan, you plan to fail"* – is equally true when it comes to personal money matters. Financial plans differ depending on where you are on life's journey. Those just starting their working years will have big picture dreams while those approaching retirement will likely have more modest aspirations.

At the end of the day, everyone wants to be happy. We all know there is some connection between money and happiness. But research shows that once you have enough money to meet your basic needs – food, clothing, shelter and maybe even an annual holiday – incremental increases in income have little effect on your happiness.

Which is why the super-rich are typically no happier than Mr. and Mrs. Average. The ultra-wealthy may have all the luxuries in the world, but they are still beset by a litany of worries. While paying the rent is not an issue, concerns about marrying gold diggers, rearing spoiled brats and feeling emotionally isolated are ever present.

Believe it or not, there is even a disease called *Wealth Fatigue Syndrome*. It afflicts wealthy individuals who feel bored and unfulfilled despite being powerful and pampered. Boredom and emptiness follow their spiral of excessive spending as they derive less and less satisfaction from bigger and bigger material indulgences in their search for thrills.

Some time ago, I read an article which suggested that money used to buy memories rather than things, creates the greatest happiness. Apparently, splurging on a vacation makes us happier than indulging on a car. Equally, taking a friend to lunch will make us happier than buying a new outfit. Now there's some food for thought!

Posting Date: 16 June 2014

Disinherit the kids

A recent philanthropy conference in Sydney did not receive a great deal of publicity. But it did discuss a topic of growing interest – how much of your wealth should you leave to your kids? Do you have an obligation to ensure that your heirs are taken care of appropriately? Or should you display a bumper sticker proclaiming, "I'm spending the kid's inheritance".

Billionaire investor, Warren Buffett, has pledged to give away 99 per cent of his wealth to charity. Microsoft founder, Bill Gates, has also declared he intends to donate his vast fortune to charity leaving his children "a minuscule portion" of his wealth. Australia's richest person, Gina Rinehart, believes her children are unfit to manage the family business and the family's wealth.

Among the super-rich, the belief in a duty to leave a big pot of gold for the next generation is waning. Andrew Lloyd Webber's five children will see little of their father's wealth as the English composer uses it to fund budding artists. Someone else who does not want suddenly-rich offspring is Nigella Lawson. The TV personality expects her children to support themselves as adults.

Spoiled rich-kids often have more money than sense which is why tycoons, celebrities and other fabulously wealthy individuals are reluctant to leave buckets of money to their broods. Not having to earn an income can ruin a person's life which is why an increasing number of wealthy parents want their progeny to develop a strong work ethic and succeed on their own.

But what about us mere mortals who are not part of the rarefied world of the super-rich? How much should we leave our loved ones? As always, opinions are divided as to the best legacy to leave behind, albeit there are fewer pieces of silver to be divvied-up from the estates of the less well-heeled.

Spending it all on yourself or bequeathing all of your worldly belongings to charity has the benefit of avoiding family inheritance feuds and fights over the fine china. Moreover, a "leave nothing" strategy stops the kids from spending your lifetime of accumulations in one fell swoop and forces them to stand on their own two feet and fend for themselves.

On the other hand, leaving an inheritance can help your kids create more meaningful lives of their own. Many parents have confidence in their children's ability to sensibly manage money and believe that an inheritance can do more good than harm. Contrary to popular wisdom, a bequest does not necessarily mean beneficiaries will become lazy, unproductive and void of ambition.

Whereas previous generations lived shorter and more frugal lives, today's baby-boomers are expected to live much longer and many intend to spend up big in their twilight years. One group – referred to as SKIs (spend kid's inheritance) – will certainly not be watching their pennies in retirement nor will they be sit-at-home grandparents with a blanket over their knees.

Rather, SKIers are determined to travel – many are grey nomads – and enjoy the fruits of their long labour. SKIers lead very active lives and many will leave no financial legacy for their children, perhaps beyond the family home. For many Gen Xers and Gen Yers, this will result in slim pickings from family estates and a smaller pie to be divided among siblings.

SKIers believe that there is absolutely no guilt attached to splurging. Personally, I don't believe that you should scrimp and save in retirement just to leave the kids the biggest inheritance possible. Equally, I am not a hedonist and so don't subscribe to spending all your money on a self-indulgent lifestyle just for the sake of it. For me, the balance lies somewhere in the middle.

The benefits of giving while you are alive should also be considered. An "early inheritance" – like helping the kids purchase a home and/or paying for the grandchildren's education – assists your family now which allows you to see the joy it brings to their lives. When you are 85, your kids will likely be approaching 60. What's the point of leaving them their entire inheritance when they are old and grey?

Finally, it's important to recognise that a legacy is not just about money. It's also about leaving the world a better place than how you found it. Your legacy speaks to the value system you lived by and the memories you created. How do you want to be remembered?

Posting Date: 29 September 2014

Social impact investing

Countries around the world are experiencing a growing gap between what society needs and what their governments can afford. Governments do not have the financial resources to solve all of the social problems facing their citizens. As a result, the business sector is increasingly playing a more active role in addressing social challenges via social impact investing.

Social impact investing is a growing field of investment that intentionally creates social impact as well as a financial return. It has been dubbed "double bottom line" investing since it generates positive outcomes for both investors and communities. Impact investing proves that the creation of economic value and social value are not mutually exclusive.

Funders to the social sector want to "do good while doing well." They seek investments that not only provide a return on investment but also target specific social needs. Some investors are willing to accept a lower financial return in exchange for the achievement of a social outcome. Importantly, both the financial and social outcomes must be measurable.

Impact investment is an international phenomenon and has attracted investors – such as private equity firms, investment funds, banks and companies – from every continent. It took a major step forward when the Social Impact Investment Forum was convened by the G8 in June 2013. UK Prime Minister, David Cameron, heralded impact investment as a "great force for social change".

Social impact investing is bringing private sector techniques to bear on public sector problems and is transforming the way we use capital and investment. It is facilitating more innovative and effective approaches to tackling critical social issues – like homelessness, affordable housing and welfare dependency – while concurrently creating economic rewards.

In 2010, the Coca-Cola Company made a strategic social investment to help fight poverty. It launched a program – called 5by20 – to empower 5 million women entrepreneurs by the year 2020. The program was initially focussed on four countries – Brazil, India, the Philippines and South Africa – and is providing women with business skills training and access to financial services.

According to Coca-Cola, women control two-thirds of spending worldwide. They also account for a disproportionately high percentage of key segments of the Coca-Cola's global value chain. For example, in the Philippines, women own or operate more than 86 per cent of the small neighbourhood stores that sell the company's products.

Women around the world have long been pillars of the Coke business system – from fruit farmers to artisans. In helping women grow their businesses, the women – in turn – help Coke grow its business, providing a win-win to both parties. Coke believes that women are a powerful but undervalued economic force and that investing in women can strengthen local communities and national economies.

Australia is one of eight countries, along with the EU, participating in the Social Impact Investment Taskforce established by the G8. Impact investing is gaining momentum here and has produced positive results in poverty alleviation and sustainable development. It is also being used to improve services for an ageing population and for Indigenous communities.

Impact investing is still in its early stages in Australia but shows great potential for growth – the market possibility in Australia is estimated to be $32 billion over the next decade. The ability to harness our nation's huge and growing pool of capital in superannuation funds for the betterment of Australia is already being discussed.

Utilising the power of business for social good is an idea whose time has come. Financial institutions have an important role to play and Gateway Credit Union intends to step up to the plate. We can't solve all of the world's problems but we can make a difference. We are currently assessing how we can become involved in impact investing and where we should direct our efforts.

Posting Date: 14 October 2014

Rethinking political correctness

Some years ago, I attended a residential university program. When I asked the course co-ordinator for the location of the campus library she politely corrected me and said, "You mean the Information Resource Centre." Eh? It's clear we no longer call a spade a spade. Just how comical things have become is evident in everyday life.

My bald friend is now referred to as "follically deprived". The drug addict down the road is "chemically dependent". The blind man on the bus is "visually impaired". The woman in the wheel chair is "physically challenged". Slow students are "developmentally delayed", bed wetters are "nocturnally compromised" and the list goes on.

The corporate world is not immune to euphemisms. Most people now know that "subprime lending" is a fancy term for high-interest loans to people who would otherwise be considered too risky for a conventional loan due to their poor credit history. Avoiding potentially offensive terminology contributed to the worst financial crisis since the Great Depression.

Hopefully, the hapless subprime borrowers and the opportunistic lenders have learned a hard lesson – all that glitters is not gold. My heart goes out to the thousands of people who lost their homes. However, I have little sympathy for the investment banks that packaged and bought the toxic mortgaged backed securities (bonds).

Attempts to mask the truth or hide unpleasantries bring into sharp focus the pitfalls of political correctness. With regard to the subprime crisis, dressing up questionable lending practices did not make them respectable. However, it seems that we all need to be sheltered from hurt or offence. Political correctness (PC) has spread like a virus and is killing free speech.

If you now say the "wrong thing" you could find yourself in hot water. Such was the fate of the UK politician who was criticised for using the phrase "nitty gritty" since it dates from the slavery era. There was also the case of the US police officer whose superiors had to defend his use of ethnic and religious words to describe a dangerous, on-the-run offender.

Not to be outdone, Australia holds its own when it comes to social engineering. In our great nation, Santa was banned from saying "ho ho ho", for fear of offending women. Sea World re-named its fairy penguins "little penguins" to avoid offending the gay community. And a member of parliament's maiden speech is now called their "first speech".

The PC onslaught has even engulfed children's nursery rhymes. In some schools, Baa Baa Black Sheep has been changed to Baa Baa Rainbow Sheep so it cannot be deemed racist. Moreover, nursery teachers have been warned that playing "musical chairs" might encourage aggressive behaviour among children.

For my money, South Australian Senator, Cory Bernardi hit the PC nail on the head in a speech, saying:

> The PC strategy is to divide and conquer, to make a public example of a few to silence the many. Many people therefore back off, scared of exposing themselves to more verbal abuse or adverse consequences should they continue to take a stand. So they are often reduced to whispering their thoughts and views with others.

It's clear that PC is running rampant throughout society and that no area has escaped its clutches. What was once acceptable is now considered offensive. Like the overwhelming majority of people, I'm all for being respectful of others and not discriminating on the basis of race, religion and gender.

Given this, should our ability to speak candidly be stifled? Should we be forced to walk on eggshells? Why can't we have meaningful and respectful discussions and agree to disagree? Isn't diversity of thought something to be cherished? I choose common sense over political correctness any day.

Posting Date: 7 October 2014

Rise of the sharing economy

If your mother is like my dear mum, she undoubtedly taught you to share. As a child, I would share things I owned, such as toys, with other kids. The term sharing is now starting to take on a whole new meaning. An increasing number of people are tapping into the sharing economy and sharing things with total strangers.

Thanks to mobile technologies we can now match those who "have" with those who "want" enabling us to rent, lend, swap and share products on a scale never before possible. It's called collaborative consumption and some believe that over time this growing movement will change the laws of supply and demand and, by extension, business models.

Collaborative consumption describes an emerging shift in consumer preferences from ownership to access via sharing. Sharing enables us to put idle assets to productive use by making money from underused assets by renting them out. Using the Internet and an iPhone, it is now possible to find people who will pay to use your dormant resources for a fraction of time.

For example, no one drives their car 100 per cent of the time, no one uses their photographic equipment 24 hours a day and many homes have spare rooms. There are now online marketplaces that enable you to link up with people who will pay to hire your motor vehicle, borrow your camera equipment or rent your empty room.

There is a growing list of collaborative consumption websites. Open Shed allows people to rent tools and other equipment. Airbnb matches people seeking short-term rentals with those with rooms to rent. GoGet gives you access to a network of locally parked cars you can hire by the hour. And Jayride enables you to share your journey while making cash via carpooling.

But wait there's more! ThredUp helps people unload or swap children's clothing and toys. Divvy connects people who want to rent out their driveway or garages with those who need to find a parking space. And SnapGoods claims it can help you borrow or rent anything from anyone. There's even a site, Shareable, which provides advice on how to build systems for sharing.

The basic premise of sharing is that owning assets can be inefficient and I can relate to this. A few years ago, I bought a power drill for a handyman job and I haven't used the drill since. It's just sitting in my garage collecting dust. If I ever need another tool, a better way for me to proceed would be to rent it for a day at say, $10, in lieu of buying it outright for $200.

Proponents of collaborative consumption say that by sharing a drill – or any item – with many other people, we use less of the planet's resources which is good for the environment. It is claimed that one shared car can take seven privately owned vehicles off the road, thereby reducing congestion and pollution.

Not surprisingly, the one issue that troubles most people about the sharing economy is trust. Can you really trust a complete stranger to respect your biggest asset (i.e., your home)? Would you trust a person you have never met to drive your second biggest asset (i.e., your car)? I certainly won't be handing the keys to my castle to total strangers!

Given the number of home-rental horror stories, I suspect that trust between strangers will remain a hot topic for some time. While I'm personally not ready to embrace many of these P2P transactions, millions of others are. I'm quite comfortable in not being an early adopter, although I'm happy to borrow the next power tool I may need for that odd job.

Posting Date: 26 May 2014

Ease your money worries

It's human to worry. Worry is a state of mind based on fear. We fear all sorts of things including rejection, failure and what may or may not occur in the future. But worrying can't change the weather or alter our height. Indeed, worrying never fixes a thing. Yet many of us spend our life in morbid anticipation of events which never actually happen.

One way to control our fears is to categorise them as either possible or probable. In theory, just about anything is possible but, in reality, not everything is probable. Sure, it's possible to die in a plane crash but it's more likely you'll suffer a fatal injury in a car accident. Equally, it's possible to be eaten by a shark but more likely you'll drown in the ocean.

Some worries, of course, are very real and understandable and not the result of phobia. An example is money worries. An increasing number of households worry about their ability to pay the bills and make ends meet. Financial angst is one of the biggest causes of stress for Australian adults.

The Global Financial Crisis (GFC) has taken its toll on relationships. Last year in Australia, divorces rose for the first time in almost a decade. Arguments about money put added stress on relationships. This is why investing in family relationships during tough times is critical. Otherwise, financial stress may destroy your family.

Paradoxically, money woes can actually increase spending habits. Some individuals go on shopping sprees to cheer themselves up even though they may be in financial crisis. But emotional spending, like emotional eating, only makes things worse. According to a recent Oxford University study, obesity is linked to money insecurity in affluent nations like Australia.

When finances are tight, other areas of life may be neglected. Therefore, during times of financial stress it's important to eat healthy foods and to get regular exercise. Physical activity stimulates the production of endorphins, the body's natural anti-depressants, which make you feel energised and positive.

Money can't buy happiness but a lack of it can set off a raft of emotional and physical problems. Let's face it, a dwindling savings account and rising debt can make the best of us sick and tired. But financial stress does not have to rule your life. Take control of your finances by preparing and sticking to a household budget.

Finally, be prepared (if necessary) to bring a little austerity into your life, no matter how hard that can be on your ego and lifestyle. Reducing debt is like losing weight – it's hard and it takes time. But financial freedom is worth the effort. And remember, don't worry, be happy.

Posting Date: 21 February 2011

What lies ahead?

Predicting the future is notoriously risky. Yet CEOs are supposed to be modern day soothsayers. Well, let me assure you, I'm no futurist. My job does not come with a crystal ball and I don't claim to have special forecasting powers. Nonetheless, having a sense of the future is critical for business.

The ability to spot new trends can reap great rewards for a company. Getting a jump on competitors can mean the difference between success and failure. Which is why innovative minds in the corporate world work overtime to gain meaningful insights about the future.

Long range vision is facilitated by predictive analytics which uses current and historical data to try and predict "what's coming next". We all know the future will not be more of the same but how will it be different? Specifically, how will the business landscape change over the next decade?

The history of predicting business trends is a tale of misjudgments. As I outlined in an earlier post, *The certainty of uncertainty*, I've always had a healthy scepticism of oracles. They offer bold proclamations which invariably turn out to be wrong.

Recently, I read an article by futurist, Thomas Frey, who claims that by 2030, "the average person in the U.S. will have 4.5 packages a week delivered with flying drones. They will travel 40 per cent of the time in a driverless car, use a 3D printer to print hyper-individualised meals, and will spend most of their leisure time on an activity that hasn't been invented yet". Hmm?

Right now, the degree of uncertainty in the business world is immense. No one really knows what the future holds, which is definitely the case in banking. But that does not stop people from making educated guesses. What we do know is that financial institutions are facing irreversible change from new technology, increased regulation and altered consumer behaviours.

According to accounting group, PwC, retail banking will look very different in 2020 than it does today. Customers will demand higher levels of service and value. Technology will change everything with biometrics (e.g., fingerprints, voice recognition) becoming commonplace in transaction authorisation.

PwC also believes that by 2020 social media will be the primary medium used by financial institutions to connect, engage, inform and understand customers. The importance of branch banking is also expected to diminish significantly as customers migrate to digital channels.

Another consulting group, Accenture, believes that banking is moving into the era of convergent disruption. This describes an environment where there is convergence between banks and other players – like telcos and start-ups – from outside the traditional banking sector.

In reality, this convergent disruption has already started. The days of banks and other financial institutions being the sole providers of banking products are over. Amazon, Facebook, Apple and Google are now competing to become part of the financial habits of their customers by developing mechanisms to effect mobile payments.

PayPal was an early mover in disrupting the payments space and now dominates online web payments, but other start-up challengers are emerging. There are those (and I'm not one of them) who believe that the cryptocurrency, Bitcoin, will prove to be the single biggest disruptor to banking and payments in the long-term.

It's clear that the way consumers will pay for goods and access funds in the future will change. The use of contactless "tap and go" technology will explode and withdrawing cash from an ATM using a smartphone will be commonplace. The security and convenience of mobile phones and thumbprints will render swipe cards obsolete.

Get ready for a brave new world of banking 'cause, as the cliché goes, "the future ain't what it used to be."

Posting Date: 15 September 2014

04.
technological

Technology is rapidly changing and expanding in every field. The gadget-filled 21st century is replete with iPhones, Kindles, laptops, tablets and electronic wallets. Technology – particularly the Internet – has transformed how we shop, how we pay for things and how we communicate. People are connected and empowered as never before with gadgets that are slimmer, faster and more energy efficient. In this final chapter, we look at, *inter alia*, the rise of technology, how to prevent cybercrime, the use of big data, the introduction of Bitcoin digital currency and the explosion in mobile banking.

Disruptive technology

The world is changing rapidly and I do my best to keep up-to-date. I particularly try to keep abreast of technological developments since they drive many of the innovations that are revolutionising the way we live and work. While almost every advance is hailed as a breakthrough, this – of course – is not the case. Picking the "next big thing" is more of an art than a science.

In hindsight, it's easy to say this or that company should have seen the winds of change coming. The harsh reality is that we really don't know which technologies will radically alter the status quo. The constantly changing corporate landscape bears witness to the repeated story of technology disrupting industries in unforeseen ways.

Who would have thought that the once mighty Kodak, a corporate icon, would disappear "in a flash"? The dominant incumbent in the camera industry for over 100 years, Kodak failed to see the threat from digital photography and this ultimately destroyed its film-based business model. Other corporate titans, like Blockbuster video and Borders bookstores, have suffered similar fates.

Big companies may be Goliaths but they are also weighed down by inertia. Newer players with disruptive technology typically bring products to the market that are simpler and more efficient than existing products. Such was the case when Apple launched its iTunes "music store" in competition to established players in the recorded music industry like Sony.

It can be seen that disruptive technologies create new competitors and undermine old business models. The $64 million question is: Will this also happen in banking? On a regular basis, we hear predictions about the death of print, the death of newspapers, the death of movie theatres and so on. Are we really going to see the death of banking as we know it?

As I opined in *Rise of mobile banking*, I don't believe so. However, there will definitely be change given the concerted attack on the payments system and other elements of the banking value chain by disrupters such as Google and Apple. If the digital disrupters get their way, a financial institution may become a mere icon on a smartphone.

There's no doubt in my mind that consumers will increasingly use mobile devices to pay for goods and services. Money's destiny is to become digital and this will give rise to the increasing use of electronic cash. To survive, the traditional banking model will have to change and along with it banks, building societies and credit unions.

It has been said that increasingly "banking is something we do rather than somewhere we go". Consumers are empowered as never before by new technologies and want better product offerings. Digital insurgents are seen to be more transparent, more flexible and more user-friendly. Traditional banking institutions need to incorporate these attributes into their value propositions.

Technology in and of itself never provides a competitive advantage. It's how technology is used to add value to the customer that's the key to success. Indeed, technology is only disruptive when it is adopted by a critical mass of people, thereby giving it broad reach and impact. Think motor vehicles displacing horse and buggies and computers displacing typewriters.

While Neil Armstrong's "small step for a man" was captured on Kodak film, banking requires a giant leap into new technology to capture tomorrow's customers. I remain confident the banking industry will move ahead with a combination of small steps and large strides and successfully reinvent itself for a marketplace which is rapidly going digital.

Posting Date: 2 December 2013

Dynamic duos change the world

Throughout history great double acts have left their mark on society. Black and Decker equipped the home handyman. Mills and Boon brought romance to the suburbs. Marks and Spencer revolutionised shopping. Gilbert and Sullivan reinvented musical theatre. And Watson and Crick unravelled the mysteries of DNA.

Perhaps no industry has given us more creative partnerships than the IT sector. Bill Hewlett and Dave Packard formed Hewlett-Packard. Bill Gates and Paul Allen started Microsoft. Steve Jobs and Steve Wozniak launched Apple. Jerry Yang and David Filo created Yahoo! And Sergey Brin and Larry Page established Google.

The unlikely pairing of the Google founders is now the subject of a book which makes fascinating reading. *Google Speaks: Secrets of the World's Greatest Billionaire Entrepreneurs, Sergey Brin and Larry Page*, is a page turner from start to finish. *Google Speaks* is an engaging account of how two Stanford University students turned a technology research project into a multi-billion dollar corporation.

Among the many interesting tidbits about Google and its founders is the fact that both Brin and Page are sons of academics and both are also mathematicians. Perhaps it's no surprise, then, that the word "Google" is a misspelling of the mathematical term "googol", which means a number represented by 1 followed by 100 zeros.

Brin and Page created a proprietary algorithm for a search engine to organise the vast amount of information available on the World Wide Web. It's estimated that Google receives several hundred million queries each day. "Google's ubiquity", according to one media writer, "has earned it the status of a verb. You don't just search for information about a person or a subject on the Web, you google it."

From its humble beginnings, Google has morphed into something much more than a search engine. Today, it's the biggest advertising platform in the world. Google offers the world's information for free but sells advertising at a hefty profit. Advertising generates 98 per cent of the company's revenues and it's now so powerful it threatens to swallow up all other media.

Savvy consumers are increasingly using the Internet to find products, investigate alternatives and compare prices. Gateway Credit Union uses Google Adwords to attract potential customers. We pay a handsome sum for each click-through. It's the cost of doing business in an online world. This year we will contribute to Google's estimated $20 billion in annual advertising revenue.

There's no doubt that Google has achieved its mission "to organise the world's content and make it universally accessible". In the process, it has redefined how business is done in a digital world. For those of you who cannot get through the day without using Google to search the Internet, *Google Speaks* is a must read.

Posting Date: 11 October 2010

Bitcoin digital currency

It's not pegged to any real-world currency. It's not issued by a government. It's not regulated by a central bank. It's not able to be used at major retailers. And it doesn't exist in a physical sense. Nonetheless, proponents of the virtual currency, Bitcoin, claim it is making its mark on the world and that it's here to stay.

Bitcoin was created in 2009 at the height of the Global Financial Crisis (GFC) by a mysterious programmer with the pseudonym, Satoshi Nakamoto, and he/she/they have now disappeared from the Internet. Born of troubled economic times, this non-governmental global currency is seen as an easy and anonymous way to transact business across borders.

This computer generated money has been on a roller-coaster ride of speculation and has attracted a fair amount of attention. The currency has faced a number of crises since it was launched and has been the subject of premature obituaries. Meanwhile, the average citizen is struggling to get their mind around how the Bitcoin digital currency works.

As a gentle lead in to this explanation, let's start with something that is familiar to most people – frequent flyer reward programs. Airline travellers are awarded points which are a form of digital currency. The points have value since they can be redeemed for goods and services. Similar to the points that are issued by airlines, they are not legal tender like normal money (i.e., fiat currency).

In contrast, Bitcoins are redeemable for fiat currency but, unlike real money, are generated via a mathematical formula – an algorithm to be precise. Using this mathematical process Bitcoins are "mined" by people called miners using Nakamoto's software. The mining is not done with a bulldozer but by computers solving complex mathematical equations.

Unlike gold, Bitcoins enter the world at a rate that shows very little variation. The algorithm that fuels the Bitcoin network ensures that the supply of Bitcoins grows at a smooth, steady pace. If mining slows, Bitcoins become easier to mine (less complex equations). If mining becomes exceedingly competitive, Bitcoin mining becomes more difficult (more complex equations).

A Bitcoin is awarded to miners each time they solve a problem. Actually solving an algorithm requires more computing power than one PC alone, so miners work together in mining pools. Each correct answer unlocks a coin which enters the Bitcoin economy. The coins emerge at a pre-determined rate and the number of Bitcoins generated will never exceed 21 million.

Each user or miner operates an electronic wallet to send, receive and store Bitcoins. The wallet address is a unique identifier, akin to an email address. A wallet address consists of a string of letters and numbers enabling the owner to remain anonymous. Bitcoins are transferred between wallets using software encryption technology to protect transactions from hackers and thieves.

No one runs Bitcoin. It is an open-source network that is not controlled by any single individual, company, organisation or government. The currency is created, traded and controlled by Bitcoin users. Being self-regulated and decentralised enables Bitcoin to process online, peer-to-peer cash payments without going through a financial institution or leaving a paper trail.

Bitcoin claims that it is untraceable and this has made it attractive to drug dealers and other criminals. Transacting via Bitcoin is also seen as a way of avoiding the tax man. However, the Australian Taxation Office is confident it can track users. In addition, the US Treasury is now applying money-laundering rules to virtual currencies, like Bitcoin.

Is Bitcoin a modern day fool's gold, or is it the currency of the future? Will this unregulated mathematical concoction replace fiat currency? Some economists regard Bitcoin as a bubble waiting to burst. Other commentators have likened it to a modern day Ponzi scheme. Many just can't make up their minds and are sitting on the fence.

Personally, I view Bitcoin as a daring economic experiment which faces formidable regulatory and security hurdles. I suspect that over time it will lose its veil of anonymity and, therefore, some of its utility and consequently its attractiveness. Moreover, I believe the wild fluctuations in its value provide a salutary caution about its volatility and unpredictability.

In the days of the barter system, stones and shells were recognised as currency. In today's world, a basic unit of information, *bit*, added to the basic unit of currency, *coin*, produce the Bitcoin currency. But is it a passing fad? As always, it's a case of buyer beware!

Posting Date: 15 July 2013

Lonely planet

The seven billion humans on this Earth are more connected than ever before. Technology has collapsed the physical boundaries between people. We are now able to communicate using a number of digital connections. The communication tools at our disposal include the telephone, Skype, text, Twitter, email, chat rooms and social media (e.g., Facebook).

We are conducting more and more of our relationships online. Technology is bringing us together but, paradoxically, it's literally keeping us apart. As we become more connected, we become more disconnected. Meeting face-to-face is being replaced by communicating keyboard-to-keyboard. It's quicker and less hassle to send a quick text message than to eyeball someone.

The line between real life and screen life has become blurred. An increasing number of people spend their days walking around with their noses buried in their BlackBerrys and iPhones. Others shut out the world with iPods. We seldom speak with our next door neighbours but "chat" incessantly with cyber friends we rarely see.

Thanks to online shopping and online communications we never have to leave home. But we do venture out because deep down we crave human touch and social interaction. For example, coffee lovers, who could make a cappuccino in their own kitchen, flock to cafés where they can sip their latte macchiato surrounded by others.

We humans are herd animals and a lack of attachment is not normal. Yet our contact with each other is becoming more and more superficial. We have broader but shallower friendships. Real flesh-and-bone friends who stick with you through thick and thin are hard to find while transient, online virtual friends seem to pop out of the cyber-world.

A real life example will help here. In 2010, a 42-year-old woman in England posted a Christmas Day suicide note on her Facebook page. Sadly, the message to her 1,082 Facebook "friends" went largely ignored. I believe the anonymity and no-social-responsibility of Facebook contributed to this tragedy. For some, social networking is a narcissistic one-way street.

Digital interaction can have unpleasant consequences. People say things over the Internet they would not dare utter to a person's face. Electronic communication allows bullies to harass victims with little risk of face-to-face confrontation. Social media provides a mask and a physical remoteness that can bring out the worst in people.

What digital communicators fail to understand is that 93 per cent of communication is non-verbal. Only 7 per cent is actual spoken words. The rest is made up of gestures, facial expressions, body language and eye contact. These elements, of course, cannot be transmitted through the Internet.

The absence of non-verbal cues is fraught with danger. Text messages can't communicate voice tone and inflection which makes it difficult to decode the sender's mood and attitudes. A funny, tongue-in-cheek remark made in person runs the risk of being misinterpreted as sarcasm when communicated in a plain text message.

Another danger with text and email messages is they can be fired off at great speed. This leaves little time for contemplation and can result in email tirades. I've seen this first-hand at Gateway Credit Union where we genuinely receive very few written complaints. The tone of the complaints we receive by snail mail is invariably more polite than the feedback contained in rapid fire emails.

For my money, digital friends will never replace real friends. I crave personal interaction with my adult children, but one lives in London, another in Singapore and yet another on the

Central Coast of NSW. While I Skype each of them weekly on a different night, I still feel short-changed because I can't hug them. Humans are tactile creatures and nothing beats spending real time with real people!

Posting Date: 18 February 2013

Mobile money revolution

There's a war going on in the mobile payments arena. Established players and fledgling start-ups are locked in a battle which rivals the 1970s VHS-versus-Betamax video format tussle. Leading-edge technology called Near Field Communications (NFC) is being pitted against tried-and-tested card/PIN technology to become the standard format for mobile payments in point-of-sale (POS) terminals.

Most of us carry our phones and wallets with us every day and this is at the heart of the attempt to combine the two into one. If proponents of NFC get their way, our leather wallets will gradually be replaced with digital wallets on our smartphones. Some believe that the emerging virtual wallet technology will completely kill off physical debit and credit cards. Well, maybe… but it won't happen overnight.

Our wallets bulge because they are full of plastic and loyalty cards. In theory, we should be able to throw away our bloated wallets as we have the technology to buy things without cards or cash. But none of the digital wallets available has taken off despite the lure of their apparent simplicity – just tap your phone against a payment terminal and go. My sense is that the magnetic stripe on the back of your plastic card won't become a relic just yet.

With "tap and go", a smartphone is used to communicate with a POS terminal via short-range wireless signals (called Near Field Communications). However, most retailers have not embraced this new technology since it's expensive to install POS terminals that can read an NFC signal from a smartphone. Without broad acceptance of tap-to-pay phone functionality at retail POS terminals, the mobile wallet will remain big on hype and small on uptake.

To add to NFC's challenge of becoming the payments standard for smartphones, Apple has not integrated NFC chips in its iPhones. These chips are used to retain bank account and credit card information and Apple's refusal to offer this functionality is seen by some as a "blatant roadblock" to NFC. In addition, PayPal president, David Marcus, is not a fan of NFC and has voiced doubts about its future.

While Marcus does not believe that tapping a phone on a terminal is any easier than swiping a credit card, others have a different view. The major Australian banks are embracing contactless payment technology and support NFC payments. A number of NFC-enabled devices running Google's Android mobile platform are available in Australia, including smartphones from Samsung.

Australia is a prime market for mobile NFC transactions because it has 70 per cent smartphone penetration. As a result, it's not surprising that MasterCard has conducted a trial of mobile payments with supermarket giant, Coles, and Visa has introduced a NFC payment app for Vodafone smartphones. Notwithstanding these developments, Apple and PayPal continue to snub NFC technology by not including it in their mobile payment offerings.

Much of the NFC debate is akin the age old chicken-and-egg problem. Retailers are reluctant to upgrade to costly NFC terminals until a critical mass of consumers has NFC technology on their phones. Meanwhile, phone makers, like Apple, have still not included NFC embedded chips in their phones since many merchants can't accept payments this way yet. Until this impasse is resolved, the widespread availability of mobile payments will remain more promise than reality.

My sense is that the take up of NFC will follow a timeline that is reflective of Bill Gates' famous quote: "The impact of all new technologies is overestimated in the short term but underestimated in the long term." For the time being, you will still need to open your wallet when paying for things. But down the track, I'm sure you'll be able to "bump" your smartphone at lots of locations – should you so desire!

Posting Date: 17 February 2014

Big data

The amount of data in our world is exploding. We are experiencing an information tsunami. According to Google CEO, Eric Schmidt, we are creating five exabytes of data (that's five with 18 zeros behind it!) every two days and the pace is increasing. To put this into some context, there was five exabytes of information created between the dawn of civilization and 2003.

The exponential growth and availability of information has created "big data" which comes from everywhere. To quote IBM, big data is sourced "...from sensors used to gather climate information, posts to social media sites, digital pictures and videos posted online, transaction records of online purchases and from cell phone GPS signals to name a few".

Traditional data analytics is used to gain insights from structured data – i.e., information that fits neatly into rows and columns like financial details. In contrast, big data analytics focusses on unstructured data such as emails, blogs, videos and photos and is used to discern trends or patterns which are not visible to the naked eye.

Many believe that society's biggest problems have answers hiding deep in the terabytes, petabytes and exabytes of the data available to us. Big data leads to small insights that can change the world. For example, by pinpointing the location of people in an earthquake zone via their SMS cards, relief agencies can rush food, water and medical supplies to where they're needed most.

Businesses are also using big data to find their own "needles in a haystack". Hidden gems of insight about consumer behaviour and preferences, which were formerly buried in a jumble of legacy systems, are being discovered using open source software such as Hadoop. Big data can now be used to support an organisation's most critical decisions.

By using big data, retailers can analyse every purchase made by every customer to identify individual spending habits. Film studios can examine the pulling power of past films to predict future Hollywood blockbusters. Airlines can also target reward offers for continued loyalty or upgrade offers to atone for service lapses such as misplaced luggage.

The use of big data is helping leading companies outperform their peers. Amazon, Google and Facebook stand out as companies that really know how to gather and utilise data. They intimately understand what makes their respective customers tick. Not surprisingly, Facebook is currently working with banks to develop social banking services on its site.

The retail banking industry is a veritable goldmine of consumer behaviour data including branch visits, call logs, web interactions, card activity and transaction types. The challenge is to extract value from these hidden repositories of data to gain actionable intelligence about customers – what and why they buy and how best to communicate with them.

What excites many executives about big data is that it puts the customer at the heart of corporate strategy. Being out of touch with the wants and needs of customers is a surefire recipe for corporate failure. Effective use of data can help organisations assist customers achieve their ambitions and support their way of life.

Of course, the ability to capture big data raises legitimate privacy concerns regarding the profiling and targeting of customers. Organisations and governments must be careful not to cross the line in the use of sensitive data. Just because the use of data is legal does not necessarily make it ethical. Data use must fall within bounds that are fair and reasonable.

The explosion of data measuring weather, traffic, health and countless other areas will transform science, medicine, finance, business and ultimately society itself. I have no doubt that big data will give rise to new categories of companies that embrace information-driven business models. Big data is set to become the new competitive advantage.

Posting Date: 28 January 2014

Rise of mobile banking

Technology continues to change our lives and, whether you realise it or not, you're part of the digital revolution. Right now you're reading this blog (a communication medium that didn't exist two decades ago) on a computer or mobile device that has more power than a typical supercomputer 20 years ago.

Smart devices – portable tools that connect to the Internet – are increasingly becoming an integral part of our lives. It is forecast that within the next 12 months more smart devices (e.g., iPhones) will be used to access the Internet than traditional computer based access.

Smartphones are changing the way we work, play and manage our money. These wireless devices are rapidly replacing desk-based computers, enabling personal money management to be done "on the fly". Today, it's common to transfer funds on your smartphone while standing in line for a cappuccino.

One of the most basic things we do as citizens of an open economy is spend – we buy goods and services and we need a way to pay for them. The number of people using banking apps to manage and pay for their spending from anywhere, 365 days a year is set to explode.

Around the world, trendsetters (early adopters) of mobile banking are being joined by a growing mass market. By the end of this year, more Australians could be dealing with their financial institution via a smartphone or tablet application than via ATM networks.

According to research by Deloitte, 30 per cent of Australians now use a mobile device to do their banking at least weekly. This is yet another example of consumers gravitating to convenience. We moved from cash to cheques then plastic cards and now we are embracing smartphones and tablets.

The merging of technology and banking is changing the competitive landscape. Banks around the world face competition from the likes of Apple and Google. These organisations are on the offensive in wanting to give consumers and merchants new payment options.

The days of banks and other financial institutions being the sole providers of banking products are over. A variety of new players, including Amazon and Facebook, is now competing to become part of the financial habits of their customers by developing mechanisms to effect mobile payments.

Apple, Google, Amazon and Facebook are often referred to as the "Gang of Four". They have collectively redefined how business is done and each has ascended to astounding heights by outwitting the competition to create a sustainable advantage.

Industry analysts believe that in a post-PC world, the Gang of Four will lead banking. As I opined in an earlier post, *The Future of Money*, it is naive to believe that banks will simply roll over and let new entrants steal their established market positions.

While I accept that the popularity of mobile payments will soar, it will not spell the end of traditional banking. Newer players, like the Gang of Four, will certainly give established institutions a run for their money. Never, however, underestimate the ability of the banking sector to fight back.

Posting Date: 23 September 2013

Design thinking

Recently, I heard someone say: "You must fail quickly and cheaply in order to learn and succeed". These words were uttered by an expert in design thinking when talking about the need to experiment with possible solutions to problems. Design thinking is an iterative process to finding solutions that requires a deep empathy for the end-user.

Design thinking has been defined as "matching people's needs with what is technologically feasible". Put simply, it melds product design with human behaviour. Steve Jobs was a proponent of design thinking which enabled him to come up with game-changing innovations like the Apple iPod. Jobs believed that design simplicity should be used to make products easy to use.

Cirque du Soleil also used design thinking to produce a breakthrough innovation. The Canadian entertainment company redesigned and repackaged the traditional circus. It created a better audience experience that is more like a sophisticated and comfortable night out at the theatre – a far cry from sitting in a cramped and smelly circus tent of old.

Businesses are increasingly using design thinking to deliver profitable, customer-focussed experiences. However, finding desirable solutions for customers using design thinking is challenging. It requires a business to look at what it does from the outside in by starting with the experience coveted by the end-user – and most businesses find that paradigm shift uncomfortable.

But deeply understanding the person or people for whom you are designing a solution can deliver transformational change. Customers must be at the heart of every business process and decision. Design thinking reframes problems through the eyes of the customer.

Financial services institutions are now embracing design thinking that is producing some novel solutions. An example is Bank of America's (BOA) *Keep the Change* Program. This was designed after the bank sent researchers into the field to observe how a customer segment behaved when spending money.

The researchers tagged along as mothers shopped and discovered that their target audience – baby-boomer women with children – rounded up their transactions for speed and convenience. The team also found that many mums had difficulty saving.

The bank presented the findings to a cross-functional team which ultimately came up with a new product. The bank launched a special Visa Debit Card that rounds up purchases to the nearest dollar and transfers the difference to the cardholder's savings account.

The convenience and ease of rounding helps BOA customers to save money over the long run. This automatic and invisible way to save is a win-win for the bank and its customers. The bank is reported to have attracted millions of new customers and billions in savings for them.

Another example of the successful application of design thinking in banking is Wells Fargo. This US bank redesigned its ATMs to create a superior user experience. The system learns what you normally do at an ATM and provides shortcuts to make routine transactions happen with a minimum of fuss.

Using predictive analytics, Wells Fargo's ATMs provide customers with an array of touch-screen buttons, based on their previous transactions and preferences. The screen layout is faster and easier with the new interface offering customers a customised experience.

There's no doubt that design thinking is an effective protocol for solving problems and discovering new opportunities. Financial institutions need to remember that customers are humans, not numbers. Finance, money and banking are part of our daily lives and those institutions that make the human connection easier will be the winners.

Posting Date: 14 July 2014

Electronic bank robbers

Thousands of Australians have become victims of identity theft. This 21st century nightmare strikes without warning and can have devastating consequences. Imagine the shock of receiving a call from a collections agency demanding immediate payment of a debt you know nothing about.

ID thieves are not visible robbers who break into your home – they are invisible hackers who maliciously attack your data. You need to make it difficult for cyberspace criminals to impersonate you since ID theft is just one mouse click away.

You should shred sensitive information rather than disposing of it in the garbage bin. You should be conscious of "shoulder surfers" when using ATMs to protect yourself from peering eyes. You should also change your password often and use passwords that combine numbers, letters and symbols.

Scam artists have acquired the ability to infiltrate IT systems with new penetration techniques, enabling them to gain undetected access to data. As mobile device functionality converges with computers, cyber criminals will increasingly target iPhones and iPads with malware (aka malicious software).

Malware includes viruses, worms, Trojan horses, spyware or any other form of unwanted software that can impact your computer's performance and stability. Malware can manifest as a simple annoyance to a serious security threat by slowing your computer to a crawl or causing it to crash totally.

It should be self-evident that in our online world your personal details are your most valuable currency. The Internet is now an integral part of the lives of most Australians, so protecting your personal information from the cyber underworld is vital.

Anti-virus software is your first line of defence against malware. You must ensure your anti-virus software is kept up-to-date.

Many people let their anti-virus software expire, thereby allowing their computer to become infected with malware. Remember, anti-virus software is only as good as the last update.

The next line of defence is to delete emails from unknown sources. Millions of email users around the world regularly receive spam – unsolicited electronic junk email. While spam from legitimate e-marketers is usually harmless, deceitful scammers prey on unsuspecting recipients.

A popular technique used by these online robbers is called phishing. Phishing enables a scammer to obtain confidential information from an Internet user by posing as a trusted authority. Users treat the spam email as legitimate and are then tricked into revealing personal information such as credit card numbers, account data, usernames and passwords.

With the help of an authentic looking but deceptive email, the attacker typically redirects the victim to a hoax or mirror website. The bogus website looks like those of a legitimate retailer or bank. The spam message typically requests the user to "update" or "validate" their account information. When clicked, the email link takes you to a copy-cat website where your personal details are illegally captured.

Therefore, another line of defence is to "click with caution". Never click on a link in a spam message or an email from someone you do not know and be wary of opening random attachments. Given the pervasive nature of spam, it's best to install spam blocking programs.

A final safeguard when using the Internet is to ascertain whether the web page you are using utilises encryption. A quick look at the address bar will reveal this. All web addresses start with the protocol "http://" which stands for Hyper Text Transfer Protocol. In simple terms, "http" can be thought of as a language for transmitting and receiving information across the Internet.

Some web addresses start with "https://". The "s" at the end stands for secure. Secure means that any information you enter is encrypted i.e., it cannot be read in free text. Your browser will also indicate whether you are transmitting over a secured https page by the indication of a lock icon. Never enter your credit card details in a http website (i.e., without the "s").

While cyber-crime represents a clear and present danger, surfing the Internet should not be a terrifying experience. You can't roll back the digital revolution but you can take routine IT hygiene steps to protect yourself online. So enjoy the benefits of our digital world while exercising common sense precautions.

Posting Date: 20 October 2014

3D printing

It's the greatest development in printing since Johannes Gutenberg invented the printing press in 1450. Three-dimensional printers have arrived and they can make copies of almost anything. 3D printing uses a process called additive manufacturing where an object is created by adding material layer-by-layer until it is fully formed.

Conventional printers fire streams of ink onto paper. In contrast, 3D "printers" use lasers to heat liquid or powdered material which is sprayed or squeezed onto a base over and over again and allowed to fuse together. The print material ("ink") used in 3D printers varies and includes metals, plastics, nylons, acrylics, ceramics, wood pulp and even chocolate.

The first step in 3D printing is to create a virtual blueprint of the object you want to print using Computer-Aided Design (CAD) software. The software analyses your design and then divides your object into cross-sections to enable the printer to build it by laying down successive layers. This can take several hours or days depending on the size and complexity of the object.

3D printing is changing the way people think about "making" things that once required industrial machines. Traditional subtractive manufacturing trims and shapes raw material to make objects, but this creates substantial waste. Additive manufacturing, on the other hand, precisely builds objects by adding raw material layer by layer so there is no waste.

In theory, every home and every business now has the ability to become a customised manufacturing plant. All you need is a 3D printer, CAD software and an Internet connection and you can design and assemble almost anything, no matter how complicated. At a household level, people have "manufactured" plates, toys, jewellery, shoes and clothing using a 3D printer.

More broadly, 3D printing has the potential to transform several industries. The main sectors to benefit to date are health, education, manufacturing and construction. In healthcare, for example, 3D printing has been used to print organ tissue from a patient's own cells. It has also been used to create hearing aids, leg braces and even a titanium jaw.

NASA is testing 3D printers that will enable Mars-bound astronauts to create a sustainable Martian colony on the Red Planet. The makers of the James Bond *Skyfall* movie turned to 3D printing to create a scale model of an Aston Martin and then burnt it for entertainment. Boeing has started using 3D printed parts for its planes, including its luxurious Dreamliner aircraft.

As with all new technology, 3D printing can have undesirable applications. It has already been used to manufacture illegal items such as weapons and to fabricate counterfeit products. An American woman was recently charged with producing counterfeit US greenbacks. This case showed how easy it is to produce bogus currency using modern technology.

One of the most high-profile criminal applications of 3D printing occurred in Sydney in 2013. A gang of Romanian criminals 3D manufactured ATM skimming devices and then targeted ATMs across Sydney, stealing around $100,000. Alarmingly, each skimming device was manufactured for a specific model of ATM so it would fit perfectly, making detection almost impossible.

Clearly, 3D printing has a dark side. When people can replicate any object with ease – like guns, drugs and house keys – you just know that some will do the wrong thing, which is why 3D printing is a double-edged sword. Its capabilities are mind blowing, producing things that defy logic. Let's just hope that the good overshadows the bad and 3D printing makes life better not worse.

Posting Date: 27 October 2014

You've got mail!

During 2012, the world's 2.2 billion email users sent an average of 144 billion emails per day. A staggering 68.8 per cent of that email traffic was spam. The average email user gets 147 messages per day and deletes 71 (48 per cent) of those messages. Office workers are estimated to spend around 28 per cent of their working day sending and receiving emails.

Fortune Magazine cites Peter Bregman, author of *18 Minutes: Find Your Focus, Master Distraction, and Get the Right Things Done*, who suggests why email management has grown from zero hours per week to 28 per cent of a person's time in a generation. "Email is such a seductress in terms of distraction because it poses as valid work," he posits, and this gives rise to avoidance behaviour.

Let's say that you are meant to be working on a business proposal, but don't feel like doing that. So you put off doing something you know you should be doing for something else – like checking your inbox. "If you could get away with watching TV, you probably would instead of writing that proposal, but you probably can't, so instead you check email," Bregman says.

Email is a double-edged sword leaving users both empowered and overwhelmed. The flood of messages is ceaseless and email has irrevocably changed our world. We need to "shut down, switch off and reconnect" with real people according to John Freeman, author of *Shrinking the world: The 4000-year story of how email came to rule our lives*.

He proposes that we try and separate ourselves from the inbox which for many has become an "electronic fidget". The compulsion to check our inboxes is akin to poker machine addiction. "Email is addictive in the same way that slot machines are addictive," says Freeman. The upshot, he warns, is that "we spend less time dealing face-to-face with other human beings and more time before a machine *playing email ping-pong*" (italics mine).

Citing a survey conducted in England, Freeman reveals that "77 per cent of office workers and company owners agree that email downtime causes major stress at work". Some psychologists are pushing to have "Internet Addiction" classified as a clinical disorder.

According to Freeman, 65 per cent of Americans spend more time with their computer than their spouse. "The computer and email were sold to us as tools of liberation, but they have actually inhibited our ability to conduct our lives mindfully," he laments.

He goes on to say that cafés used to be filled with people talking to one another or reading books or newspapers. You will now find people sitting alone before the glowing screen of their laptop, typing emails, working on documents and chatting with friends online.

Freeman sees electronic messages as "completely devoid of sensuality," noting that we misunderstand the tone of emails 50 per cent of the time. This is not a surprise, says Freeman, as "there is no face on the other end to … indicate that what we are in the process of saying is rude, not comprehended or cruel".

The growing absence of face-to-face communication has given rise to cyber-crime. Freeman identifies phishing, spam, cyber-bullying and ID theft as examples of miscreant activities. He also identifies a new form of narcissism, ego-surfing, in which "one searches the Internet for information about oneself".

Like Freeman, I believe that between the carrier pigeon and the inbox, communication lost its personality. While I'm not suggesting we go back to smoke signals, there's still a place for phone and face-to-face communication. The tone and inflection of your voice and the smile on your face means it's less likely the receiver will misinterpret your message. Try it!

Posting Date: 17 November 2014

Young and rich

The world is changing and nowhere is this more apparent than wealth creation. In bygone days, it took decades of hard work to amass your riches. A young tech-savvy website designer or app developer can now become a millionaire seemingly overnight.

By mastering the art of Internet commerce, this new breed of web entrepreneurs is capitalising on the tech revolution. They are striking it rich by solving problems and being catapulted into extreme wealth. The road to riches typically starts at a young age by forming a small technology company.

The pin-up boy for tech start-ups is Facebook CEO, Mark Zuckerberg. This 30 year old Harvard dropout is reportedly worth $33.3 billion and became a billionaire at age 23. He co-founded Facebook when he was a teenager. It changed how millions of people around the world communicate.

Although no longer considered young, Google co-founders, Sergey Brin and Larry Page (both 41) achieved their game-changing idea of organising the world's information and making it universally accessible. In the process, they became very wealthy and are worth a head-spinning $31.8 billion and $32.3 billion respectively.

Perhaps today's young whiz-kids take their inspiration from another technology innovator, Bill Gates. The Microsoft founder recently regained the mantle of the world's richest person. Despite his efforts to give truckloads of his fortune away, Gates – according to *Forbes Magazine* – still has $76 billion at his disposal.

It seems that the key to success for young technology entrepreneurs is to be a trendsetter who is ahead of the curve. If you can come up with the next big idea and have the drive to succeed, you could find yourself suddenly rich and famous before you are even old enough to vote.

Such is the case with 17-year-old British teenager, Nick D'Aloisio, who last year sold his iPhone app Summly to Yahoo for $30 million. The app uses an algorithm to pull in news articles from various sources and then creates a 400-character summary which is delivered to your phone.

In Australia, the search is on for a locally grown Mark Zuckerberg. Is the creator of the next Facebook or indeed the next Apple or Amazon hiding in our ranks? One of the world's most successful venture capital funds has spent almost $US20 million trying to find out.

Meanwhile, we already have a number of success stories. The *BRW Magazine* recently published a Young Rich List 2014 of the wealthiest Australians under 40. In line with worldwide trends, technology was the most dominant sector on the Young Rich List, taking 30 spots.

Sitting on top of the rich heap are local tech boys made good – Mike Cannon-Brookes and Scott Farquhar – with a combined wealth of $2.1 billion. The former university mates have been referred to as "accidental billionaires" since they never set out to be rich.

In 2002, the pair co-founded Atlassian software when they were both 22 and have become software titans. Their software is used by many of the world's largest companies. Their products include project planning software as well as information sharing and collaboration software.

It's clear that in the 21st century wealth is being created faster than ever before via technology. So, if you have a bright young software wunderkind at home, tell him/her to forgo the safety of a desk job and go out and develop an app. You never know – his/hers may be the next rags to riches story.

Posting Date: 24 November 2014

Digital revolution

Have you ever heard of Moore's law? It's not a law of physics but a guiding principle of the high-tech industry. The term was coined by Intel co-founder Gordon Moore in 1965. In computing, Moore's law states that the number of transistors on a chip doubles every 24 months. Put simply, Moore's law posits that technology will double in power every two years.

Moore's law quickly makes last year's laptop models outmoded and means that next year's technology devices will be smaller and faster than today's. You can see the results of Moore's law all around you in the devices we use every day including personal computers, laptops, mobile phones and consumer electronics.

The technology that we now have at our fingertips would have been unimaginable a few decades ago. The PC on your desk is more powerful than a typical supercomputer 20 years ago. Moreover, your mobile phone has more computer power than Apollo 11 did back in 1969 when NASA sent three astronauts to the moon.

Digital technology has generated new wealth, revolutionised the world economy and altered the way we live and work. Advances in communication and information technology have irreversibly changed the pace and face of business. Most companies today operate an e-commerce platform making it easier for them to do business both nationally and internationally.

Who would have thought a decade ago that iPads and mobile phones would have such a profound impact on business strategy? The pace of technological change has been swift and even greater innovations are on the horizon.

According to a recently released report from Deloitte Access Economics, Australian businesses must equip themselves to deal with the changing digital landscape or risk losing market share to more nimble competitors. The report, *Digital disruption*

– *Short fuse, big bang?*, predicts that one-third of the economy faces imminent disruption by digital technologies.

The six industries it puts directly in the firing line include the finance sector which is expected to experience the most significant digital disruption in the short term. Industries/companies that are likely to experience significant digital disruption within the next three years are said to be on a 'short fuse'. The magnitude of the impact of that fuse is described as the 'bang'.

Deloitte says the 'short fuse, big bang', scenario presents both threats and opportunities for business. The report notes that "digital opens up unprecedented possibilities. These innovations are changing economies and markets, and reinventing relationships between organisations, suppliers and customers. They are changing society."

On the other side of the coin, not everyone will be a winner from the digital revolution. "Digital reduces barriers to entry, blurs category boundaries, and opens doors for a new generation of entrepreneurs and innovators. In turn, incumbent market leaders will face substantial pressures."

Digital disruption will also affect the workforce with some jobs disappearing while others will be created. Furthermore, new technology will alter the way people are recruited, trained and deployed. Smartphones, tablets and home computers will provide organisations with "the opportunity to shift from traditional enclosed, hierarchical workforces to networked and distributed models".

The Deloitte report is a timely reminder that organisations and individuals must embrace the digital age or risk being left behind. "It's vital to recognise that when it comes to digital disruption, the biggest risk may in fact be doing nothing at all." As always, it's clear that inaction is not a viable option.

Posting Date: 1 October 2012

Online identity verification

My name is Paul Thomas and I can prove it. I can show you a passport with my name and photograph. I can also provide you with a driver's licence with my name and picture. I can flash any number of plastic cards with my name. Plus, I have a raft of commercial documents which bear my moniker and residential address.

In the physical world in which we live, it's not difficult to establish who you are. But in the online world, it's a different story. Some people do not reveal their true identities, preferring to use nicknames and other pseudonyms. Other Internet users represent themselves visually by choosing an avatar, an icon-sized graphic image.

Being anonymous on the web by adopting a fake identity is common. Advocates believe that having a secret digital identity is a good thing as it enables people to speak freely. Victims of abuse, whistle-blowers exposing wrongdoings and citizens of oppressive regimes will speak out without fear of repercussions, so the argument goes, if they are unidentifiable.

There is, however, a very destructive side to Internet users operating incognito. Utilising a behind-the-mask persona can give rise to "thuggish anonymity" and "faceless vitriol" and manifests itself in the form of bullying, racism and trolling. Internet trolling is defined as "the anti-social act of causing interpersonal conflict and shock-value controversy online."

Most cybercrime is committed by individuals or small groups who operate with fake identities. Malware code writers create viruses, worms, Trojans and spyware under the cover of anonymity. Meanwhile, computer hackers use the veil of the Internet to launch devastating attacks on the computers of public and private sector organisations.

Not surprisingly, such cloak-and-dagger deception has led to a push to eliminate concealed online identities. A growing chorus is calling for more transparent and robust procedures to establish the bona fides of Internet users. Verification of online identity has become much more important given the exponential rise in electronic commerce.

While sites like Google and Facebook have 'real name only' policies, the days of Internet anonymity are far from over. As always, there is disagreement among governments on how to solve the problem. Much of the debate centres on balancing the need to protect privacy on the one hand while preventing cybercrime on the other.

For European countries, the solution is a government-issued electronic ID card. Finland was the first to provide these in 1999. Estonia followed in 2002 and Belgium in 2003. According to *The Economist* magazine, 16 European states now offer their citizens electronic ID. The e-cards, which can include biometric data, authenticate users of online services.

In India, where many citizens lack any form of identity, the government has followed the European model. India has registered 275 million of its 1.2 billion people in one of the world's most sophisticated ID schemes (it includes iris scans and fingerprints). The target is to have 600 million Indians with secure online identity by 2015.

Meanwhile, other countries are wary of introducing a single, centrally run identity register. Australia and America, for example, do not have a national identification card because the electorate in both nations fears it would lead to a police state. While concerns about Big Brother are understandable and run deep, they should not stop nations from protecting innocent citizens.

Each year, a growing number of people are victims of cybercriminals. Cyber stalkers, computer hackers, card fraudsters, virus disseminators, information phishers, software pirates, email scammers and online pedophiles hide behind the anonymity afforded by the Internet to avoid detection and get away with crimes that could be largely prevented.

I have no doubt that the day will come when it will be illegal to log onto the Internet without providing proof of identity. This simple step will significantly curb the activities of miscreants who sabotage the integrity of the World Wide Web. Until that time, my fear is that digital crime will (unnecessarily) rise as the bad guys in this electronic battle are allowed to fly under the radar to escape detection.

Posting Date: 4 March 2013

Afterword

Please allow me to begin this ending with an adage from legendary English writer, Samuel Johnson: "A writer only begins a book. A reader finishes it." Thank you for getting to the end of this book. Dr Johnson also said that "the two engaging powers of an author are to make new things familiar and familiar things new." I hope I have done just that.

The tale of how *Bite size advice* came to be can be traced back to late 2007. At that stage, Gateway Credit Union was redesigning its website and my then Head of Marketing, Loyce Cox-Paton, informed me that the new site would have provision for a CEO blog. My immediate response was to ask – what's a blog?

I was told that a blog is a form of self-publishing which enables you to share your thoughts and ideas with people online via a publicly accessible journal. After I digested what that meant, I said, "Thanks, but no thanks." But Loyce persisted and I reluctantly agreed to start blogging. My first blog post was published on 25 March 2008 and is reproduced here:

I must confess to feeling a tad nervous. I'd never heard of a blog 12 months ago. Yet here I am today sharing my thoughts publicly. I've always considered myself a frustrated writer, so I'm happy to accede to the wishes of my executive colleagues and give blogging a go.

I've had a crash course in blogging and think I understand the rules of the game. It's been drilled into me that CEO blogs are not for corporate spin but for honest opinions. My aim is to write my blogs in a conversational style to facilitate open, two–way communication.

The danger that all leaders face is receiving only filtered feedback. With the best of intentions, sometimes the bad news does not get to the CEO. Of course, the real boss in any organisation is the customer and I'm keen to hear from our members and potential members.

So, please use this new communication medium to tell me what you think. I have broad shoulders, so you can be frank. If we've made a mistake or fallen short in our service delivery, I'll unreservedly apologise. However, I'll draw the line at feedback which is unnecessarily rude or profane.

Well, I have never received offensive feedback on my blog and my readership continues to grow. A new reader to my blog about three years ago was Katherine Owen. Katherine and I met a short time earlier at an industry event and following that she subscribed to my blog.

I caught up with Katherine in the latter part of 2014 and she serendipitously informed me that she had started her own publishing company. Harbouring a life-long desire to publish,

I seized the opportunity and asked Katherine if she would consider publishing the blog in book format and to my delight she agreed.

The first step in the blog to book process was obtaining the approval of my board of directors. My blog is not a personal blog but a corporate blog, written by me in my capacity as CEO of Gateway Credit Union. I thank the board for approving my request and acknowledge each of my directors viz, Catherine Hallinan, John Flynn, Steve Carritt, Mal Graham, Graham Raward and Rene van der Loos.

Little did I know that the next step on the road to publishing would be so difficult. Katherine told me that the ideal word count for my book was 50,000 to 60,000 words. That meant I had to cull about 200 of the 300 blog posts I had written. The culling process straddled a three week period and occurred in three stages. At the end of the third cull, I was within Katherine's word count limit.

My final challenge was to sort the remaining 100 posts into common themes so that they could form chapters. My first two attempts at sorting the blogs into subject categories proved futile. Then, after a week of quiet reflection and contemplation (to keep a lid on my frustration!), the answer hit me – sort the blog posts using a PEST framework.

For the uninitiated, a PEST analysis is a simple and widely used tool that helps a business to evaluate the impact that Political, Economic, Social and Technological issues may have on its operations. To my delight, I found that the blog posts could be categorised into one of the four PEST areas and these became the thematic book chapters.

I continue to blog and publish a new post every Monday morning (Sydney time). Those readers wishing to follow my blog and receive the latest blog content can do so using the RSS subscription button at www. gatewaycu.com.au/CEOBlog.

Resource List

This resource list acknowledges my debt to the many and varied sources of data and ideas I drew upon in researching and writing the 100 blog posts contained in this book. The list is arranged under the medium of publication and each citation includes sufficient information – including a URL where appropriate – to allow that source to be located and retrieved.

BOOKS

Benyus, Janine M. 1997. *Biomimicry: Innovation Inspired by Nature.* New York: HarperCollins Publishers.

Collini, Stefan. 2010. *That's Offensive!: Criticism, Identity, Respect*. Calcutta: Seagull Books.

Collins, Jim. 2001. *Great To Good: Why some companies make the leap...and others don't*. Sydney: Random House.

Easterly, William. 2007. *The White Man's Burden: Why The West's Efforts To Aid The Rest Have Done So Much Ill And So Little Good*. New York: Penguin Books.

Ehrlich, Paul R. 1968. *The Population Explosion*. New York: Buccaneer Books.

Fisher, Roger and Ury, William and Patton, Bruce. 1991. *Getting to Yes: Negotiating an agreement without giving in*. Sydney: Random Century Australia.

Freeman, John. 2009. *Shrinking the world: The 4000-year story of how email came to rule our lives*. Melbourne: Text Publishing Company.

Gardner, Dan. 2011. *Future Babble: Why Expert Predictions Fail – and Why We Believe Them Anyway*. Melbourne: Scribe Publications.

Greenleaf, Robert K. 2002. *Servant Leadership: A Journey into the Nature of Legitimate Power & Greatness*. 25th anniversary edn. New Jersey: Paulist Press.

Honoré, Carl. 2005. *In Praise of Slow: How a Worldwide Movement is challenging the Cult of Speed*. London: Orion Books.

Moyo, Dambisa. 2010. *Dead Aid: Why Aid Is Not Working And How There Is Another Way For Africa*. Melbourne: Penguin Books.

Porter, Michael E. 1990. *The Competitive Advantage of Nations*. New York: The Free Press.

Provine, Robert R. 2001. *Laughter: A Scientific Investigation*. Melbourne: Penguin Books.

Sachs, Jeffrey. 2005. *The End of Poverty: How We Can Make It Happen In Our Lifetime*. Melbourne: Penguin Books.

Shiller, Robert J. 2005. *Irrational Exuberance*. 2nd edn. Princeton, NJ: Princeton University Press.

Shiller, Robert J. 2008. *The Subprime Solution: How Today's Global Financial Crisis Happened, and What To Do about it*. Princeton NJ: Princeton University Press.

Taleb, Nassim Nicholas. 2007. *The Black Swan: The Impact of the Highly Improbable*. Melbourne: Penguin Books.

Tanner, Lindsay. 2011. *Sideshow: dumbing down democracy*. Melbourne: Scribe Publishing Pty Ltd.

Tapscott, Don and Williams, Anthony. 2008. *Wikinomics: How Mass Collaboration Changes Everything*. Great Britain: Atlantic Books.

Thaler, Linda Kaplan and Kovel, Robin. 2007. *The Power Of Nice: How To Conquer The World With Kindness*. Sydney: Allen Unwin.

Tuckett, David. 2011. *Minding the Markets: An Emotional Finance View of Financial Instability*. UK: Palgrave Macmillan.

Valenzuela, Michael J. 2011. *Maintain Your Brain: What you can do to improve your brain's health and avoid dementia*. Sydney: HarperCollins Publishers.

Weatherford, Jack. 1997. *The History of Money*. New York: Three Rivers Press.

MAGAZINES & PERIODICALS

Klein, Paul. 2011. 'Three Great Examples of Shared Value in Action'. *Forbes* (online). 14 June. Available: www.forbes.com/sites/csr/2011/06/14/three-great-examples-of-shared-value-in-action/

Lewis, Michael. 2010. 'Beware of Greeks Bearing Bonds'. *Vanity Fair* (online). October. Available: www.vanityfair.com/news/2010/10/greeks-bearing-bonds-201010

Popelka, Larry. 2012. 'Made in China Olympic Uniforms are a Win for the U.S'. *Bloomberg Business, The Management Blog*. 16 July. Available: www.bloomberg.com/bw/articles/2012-07-16/made-in-china-olympic-uniforms-are-a-win-for-the-u-dot-s-dot

Vanderkam, Laura. 2012. 'Stop checking your email, now'. *Fortune* (online). 8 October. Available: www.fortune.com/2012/10/08/stop-checking-your-email-now/

'Identity providers: The voucher business'. *The Economist*. 9 February, 2013. Available www.economist.com/news/international/21571418-which-firms-will-profit-proving-your-identity-online-voucher-business

'The euro deal: No big bazooka'. *The Economist*. 29 October 2011. Available: www.economist.com/node/21534851

NEWSPAPER ARTICLES

Gallop, Geoff. 2011. 'When populism raises its ugly head'. *The Age* (online). 1 February. Available: www.theage.com.au/federal-politics/political-opinion/when-populism-raises-its-ugly-head-20110131-1aaw7.html

Jericho, Greg. 2013. 'Australia is rich and on top of the world: is it time to pop the champers?'. *The Guardian* (online). 14 October. Available: www.theguardian.com/business/grogonomics/2013/oct/14/australia-wealth-top-world

Stiglitz, Joseph. 2013. 'Australia, you don't know how good you've got it'. *The Sydney Morning Herald* (online). 2 September. Available: www.smh.com.au/comment/australia-you-dont-know-how-good-youve-got-it-20130901-2sytb.html

BUSINESS PUBLICATIONS

Deloitte Touche Tohmatsu Limited. 2012. 'Digital disruption: Short Fuse, Big bang'. September. Available: www2.deloitte.com/content/dam/Deloitte/au/Documents/Building%20Lucky%20Country/deloitte-au-consulting-digital-disruption-whitepaper-0912.pdf

Deloitte Touche Tohmatsu Limited. 2012. 'The future of exchanging value: Uncovering new ways of spending'. July. Available: www2.deloitte.com/content/dam/Deloitte/au/Documents/technology/deloitte-au-tech-future-exchanging-Value-161014.pdf

Deloitte Touche Tohmatsu Limited. 2014. 'Get out of your own way: Unleashing productivity'. October. Available: www2.deloitte.com/content/dam/Deloitte/au/Images/infographics/au-deloitte-btlc-get-out-of-your-own-way.pdf

INTERNATIONAL DOCUMENTS

OECD. 2008. 'Growing Unequal? Income Distribution and Poverty in OECD Countries'. October.

OECD. 2011. 'Divided We Stand: Why inequality Keeps Rising'. December.

RESEARCH REPORTS

Oxfam Briefing Paper. 2014. 'Working For The Few: Political capture and economic inequality'. 20 January. Available: www.oxfam.org/sites/www.oxfam.org/files/bp-working-for-few-political-capture-economic-inequality-200114-summ-en.pdf

CONFERENCE PAPERS

Rafe, Barry and Howes, Melinda. 2012. 'Living Until 120: The Implications for Absolutely Everything'. Paper presented to the Actuaries Institute Financial Services Forum, Melbourne, May. Available: www.actuaries.asn.au/Library/Events/FSF/2012/FSF2012PaperHowesRafe.pdf

About the Author

P aul Thomas has worked in the financial services industry for almost 40 years. His journey from bank teller to credit union CEO began in 1976. He followed an old-fashioned career path that saw him rise through the ranks. Along the way, he gained broad experience in retail banking across a range of financial institutions.

Versed in all aspects of management, Paul is a high calibre executive with particular expertise in strategy development and execution. His deep knowledge of contemporary issues coupled with his passion for communication find expression in his weekly blog. He writes respectfully and insightfully – but without fear or favour – for the public at large.

Paul has developed a reputation as a thought leader and commentator on the contemporary political, economic, social and technological issues facing business and society. He offers informed insights and opinions in an authoritative voice that is authentic and engaging.

An accomplished public speaker and writer, Paul's credentials include an MBA and a Diploma in Financial Services.